MANAGING RECRUITMENT AND SELECTION

by Gill Taylor

Goldsmiths
UNIVERSITY
OF LONDON

Centre
for Public and
Voluntary Sector
Development

A Directory of Social Change publication

MANAGING PEOPLE

by Gill Taylor

Published by the Directory of Social Change, 24 Stephenson Way, London NW1 2DP, from whom further copies can be obtained. *Tel:* 0171 209 5151; *Fax:* 0171 209 5049.

E-mail: info@d-s-c.demon.co.uk to place orders or to obtain a full catalogue of other books available, with order form.

ISBN 1 873860 85 4

British Library Cataloguing in Publication Data

A catalogue record for this book is available from the British Library

Designed and typeset by Paul Ticher

Printed and bound in Britain by Page Bros., Norwich

CONTENTS

Appointment

Further reading

Appendices

INTRODUCTION

Getting the right people in post at the right time is a crucial aspect of management. All managers are likely to have to recruit at some point in their careers, some very regularly. As it costs at least £1500 (and sometimes up to £3000) to get a new staff member in post and trained up, it is a decision that must be made to the best of a manager's abilities. Mistakes in recruiting or where posts have a high turnover of staff are very expensive for organisations.

This book is aimed at people who are relatively new to management or who want to review their skills in recruitment and selection. The scenarios feature primarily paid staff but could be just as useful for committee members or other people who are involved in selection.

The book aims to demystify the skills of recruitment, selection and appointment of staff, by looking at some fairly typical difficulties that face managers. I hope that in using this book you will feel more skilled and confident in knowing that you are getting the best staff possible, using an equalities approach.

The scenario format is used throughout the book to make the subject interesting and lively and so that the dilemmas feel 'real' rather than academic. All the organisations and problems covered are inventions and not taken from real life. Any similarities are purely co-incidental.

In total there are 31 scenarios showing different problems and decisions faced by managers. At the end of the book there is a resource section of useful books and addresses. There are also examples of the forms most commonly used in recruitment.

The information in this book is for guidance only, and is not a substitute for legal advice. The legal information is as accurate as possible at the time of writing, December 1995.

The book features three managers of different organisations and their teams. While each scenario is self-contained, some follow on from each other, taking the same characters working through an issue over time.

Each scenario follows the managers through the actions they take to deal with an issue, shows what options they might have had and the consequences of the actions they took.

CARMEL

is the director of *RESCROFT*, a service for people with learning difficulties, which operates three residential projects and an outreach service. There are a total of 40 staff. Carmel directly manages:
  • 4 Project Managers: Dipak, Joseph, Kate and Ingrid
  • the Finance Manager: Luis
  • the new Deputy Manager: Daria
  • a part-time Administration Worker: Ethel

ADAM

is the manager at *ALCOHOL COUNSELLING SERVICE* (ACS), an advice and counselling centre on alcohol abuse. Paul is chair of the Management Committee. Adam manages six permanent staff:
  • 3 Advisers: Torben, Anat and Eva
  • 1 Secretary/Administrator: Judy
  • 1 Information Worker/Researcher: Kostas then Martha
  • 1 Finance Worker: Florence
and 6 further sessional counsellors

SIAN

is the director of *NATIONAL ORGANISATION OF HEALTH PROMOTION* (NOHP). NOHP had three staff until it recently acquired a large grant and has since grown quickly. It uses external consultants on the development of new projects and secondees from the Council and from business. Chair of the Management Committee is Brian, committee members Jean and Barbara. Among the staff are:
  • Researcher: Nualla
  • Information Co-ordinator: Julia
  • Development Worker: Sohalia

Since the issuing of a contract is not specifically covered in any of the scenarios, readers may find this summary useful.

Under the **Employment Protection (Consolidation) Act 1978** and the **Trade Union Reform and Employment Rights Act 1993**, the employer must give a **written statement of employment particulars** within the first two months of employment to every employee who will work more than one month. A good employer will give all employees a written statement within the first few days of employment (even if the worker is on a probationary period).

Even if the employer does not give a written statement, a contract of service (or employment) is assumed to exist in law. It exists as soon as an offer of work is given and accepted, and may include:

- anything in the job advert, job description or other written information about the job.
- anything included in the job application or in the letter of appointment, or promised at the job interview.
- the minimum requirements and obligations set out in various legislation, e.g. regarding period of notice.
- terms which are part of every contract of employment even though they are hardly ever written down **(implied terms)**, for example an obligation to follow statutory requirements.

The written statement of employment particulars must include:

- Name of employer
- Name of employee
- Job title or brief description of the job
- Starting date of employment, and whether this employment is continuous with any previous employment
- If the job is not permanent, the period for which the employment is expected to continue or, if it is for a fixed term, the date when it is to end
- Place of work (or an indication that work is or may be in more than one place, and the employer's address)
- Rate of pay, including overtime and bonuses
- Pay period
- Hours of work
- Holiday entitlement and holiday pay
- Sickness entitlement and sick pay arrangements
- Pension rights
- The amount of notice the employee and employer must give to terminate employment

- Name or job title of person to whom the employee should go with a grievance
- If there are 20 or more employees, the grievance procedure or where the employee can see the written procedure
- Details of any relevant collective agreements.

This is only the legal minimum. Employees have other automatic legal rights, which it is good practice to include in the contract.

A NOTE ON PART-TIME WORKERS

To comply with European legislation, part-time employees — defined as those who work less than 16 hours per week — have had since February 1995 virtually all the same employment rights as those who work more than 16 hours. Most significantly, all employees are now able to claim unfair dismissal or redundancy payments after two years continuous service. (The two-year period is currently before the House of Lords, and is likely to be reduced to one year for unfair dismissal.)

This change arose because more women than men work part-time, and it was therefore held to be unfair sex discrimination to have different requirements for part-time workers. However, maternity rights were not changed as a result of this decision, because they apply only to women, and so any differentials cannot be sex discrimination. Therefore employees who work less than 16 hours per week must still work for five years to get the same maternity benefits that those who work 16 or more hours per week get after only two years.

ABOUT THE AUTHOR

Gill Taylor is the senior management consultant of Connections Partnership, specialising in personnel and equality management. She has fifteen years' experience of working in and consulting to the voluntary sector.

Her particular interests are: working with managers and committees to design effective roles and jobs in organisations; working with teams on managing diversity and managing conflict.

She is a qualified Member of the Institute of Personnel and Development, and has written several other books on personnel and equal opportunities.

1 JOB DESCRIPTIONS

How to decide the best way to fit work into jobs

The work of the whole Administration & Finance department of RESCROFT no longer fits the jobs and job descriptions of the postholders. The organisation has doubled in size in two years, but the Administration & Finance department has increased by only two part-time workers. Luis manages the department, which has a full-time finance worker, part-time administrator and part-time receptionist/secretary. They are all overstretched. Carmel, the director, is aware of the difficulties in the department and has had it in mind for at least six months to assess what work needs to be done and how to get it done. Now Ethel, the part-time administrator, has said she is leaving; partly because she wants to work full-time and partly because of the stress of her post at RESCROFT. Carmel feels guilty about not having been able to prioritise sorting out the team before now, and feels she has let them all down.

Should Carmel: **OPTIONS**

- get in a consultant to carry out an organisational review?
- carry out an exit interview plus some other diagnostic work herself and come up with a plan for the department with Luis?
- apologise to Ethel and try to find the money to increase the administrator's hours to full time?

When a post becomes vacant in your organisation, you can take the **ISSUES**
opportunity to assess whether the role of the post has changed and how you can best get the work done. The process used to clarify this is by collecting information from job analyses and exit interviews (see the following scenario). It can also be done from scratch for new posts. Then you can decide how to get the work done, whether it all fits into one job or not, how flexible you can be about getting it done, whether to recruit or not, what work to put into the new post, and which bits can be done in different ways. If the organisation has grown beyond its original structure in more than one department, it may make sense to organise a full organisational review.

PLANNING Carmel consults Luis and the chair of the Management Committee and decides that a review is in order, but that they can do it themselves. They inform the whole department that they will be carrying out the job analysis and looking at all the roles in the department. They make it clear that no one will lose their jobs or be made redundant as a result of the process. As a result of the review there may be additional roles planned for the department that existing staff may want to apply for.

ACTION Carmel and Luis decide to use some of the reserves to upgrade the administrator job to full-time and offer it to Ethel, pending a review of all the work and posts in the Administation & Finance department. Ethel declines and says she'd rather move on anyway. They get in a locum full-time administrator for six months pending the result of the review.

Carmel carries out an exit interview with Ethel and interviews all the other staff to find out what they do and whether it relates to their existing job descriptions, and where the pressure areas are. She discusses the results with Luis and draws up a new departmental plan which:

- updates all the job descriptions to reflect accurately what staff are doing.
- lists all the pressure areas.
- considers the role of the Administration & Finance department in the light of future planned growth of RESCROFT including two new projects over the next two years.
- makes recommendations for new roles in the department over a period of time.
- considers regrading of salary scales in the light of the findings.
- makes a plan for immediate changes and timed changes over the next two years.

OUTCOME This has taken Carmel the best part of five days work, which she has fitted into her schedule over four weeks. She thinks it has been well worth it, and has raised morale enormously in the department. Luis is now smiling rather than looking stressed all the time.

Carmel has discovered that the personnel administration work that was part of Ethel's job could easily form the basis of a full-time post.

The shape of the department after two years of existence will now be as shown overleaf.

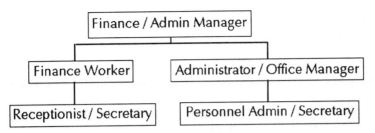

The Personnel Administrator and Receptionist will work closely together, cover for each other and share tasks when necessary. The personnel management function will be centralised at head office and each manager will work with the Personnel Administrator to sort out recruitment. The post of Administration & Finance Manager may be split into two in the long run, but the full-time Administrator will take more burden off Luis, so that he can do more of the financial planning necessary in an increasingly complex organisation.

The new post will be funded out of the contract bids to the Council and Health Authority.

All organisations end up with staff/work imbalances from time to time, especially when they are growing. Carmel made good use of the fact that one worker was leaving to analyse what was going on and plan for the future. This need not wait until someone leaves, but can be carried out with workers in post. **COMMENT**

The point of job analysis is to check if the post and job description are still the best for the organisation or whether things have changed enough to warrant a review. It is a good discipline to get into.

In this case it led to a departmental review being appropriate as well, but this need not happen every time. However, changing the emphasis of one job may well lead to changed working relationships.

TIPS ON JOB ANALYSIS

- Take the time to plan and think about each vacancy.
- Describe accurately the requirements and duties of the job.
- Decide whether to reallocate the work within the existing workforce or whether to recruit new staff.
- Don't just fill the job without carrying out a review.
- Don't ignore opportunities to introduce flexible working.

NEXT STEP Carmel plans to include job analysis as part of the personnel checklist for each post.

WHAT IS JOB ANALYSIS? Job analysis is the process of collecting and analysing information about the tasks, responsibilities, performance standards, working conditions and working relationships of jobs.

The information to be collected as part of job analysis varies to some extent with the purpose for which it is being done, but the following categories of basic information are usually found:

1. *Job identification data:* Job title, department, organisation name, location.

2. *Relationships with others:* Reporting relationships, supervisory relationships, liaison internal to the organisation, contacts and liaison outside the organisation, co-ordinating relationships.

3. *Job content:* Actual tasks or duties, level of responsibility for tasks, importance of tasks, how often performed.

4. *Working conditions:* Physical environment; social environment, such as working alone or in a group; usual time of work; economic environment such as salary and benefits.

5. *Performance standards or objectives:* These can either be for the job as a whole or for specific tasks. They can be expressed in quantitative terms such as raising £X per annum or qualitative terms such as maintaining group cohesiveness.

So the end result of job analysis will be information for:
- the job description.
- the person specification.
- performance standards for use in staff supervision and appraisal, discipline and grievance procedures, monitoring and evaluation.
- reporting relationships for accountability.
- contacts and liaison relationships internal and external to the organisation.
- working conditions particular to the post.

2 EXIT INTERVIEWS

What to do when your staff leave

One of the project workers in the eldercare project at RESCROFT is leaving. The turnover in that post is high and Carmel wonders if there is something about the post or the project she is missing that makes the job unduly difficult. She consults the Personnel subgroup of the Management Committee on what to do. One of the members from a larger organisation suggests that RESCROFT should adopt exit interviews, as a means of finding out about the reasons for leaving and what workers are dissatisfied with. If the issues are structural or managerial, then the organisation can do something to make it more likely that the staff turnover will decrease. Carmel has heard about exit interviews, but is dubious about their value; she wonders if they might just provide an opportunity for carping or griping.

Should Carmel: **OPTIONS**

- ignore the Management Committee member as interfering in her management style?
- give the exit interview an exploratory trial in this case and see if anything useful comes out of it?
- discuss the issue at the managers' meeting for comments and ideas?

- *The purpose of an exit interview with an outgoing employee is to*   **ISSUES**
  find out the reason(s) for leaving and if there are any implications for the future management of the post or the organisation.
- *An outgoing employee might provide useful information for future design of the job, the job description and the person specifications.*
- *Some employees might be tempted to use the occasion as an opportunity to stir things up for whatever reasons of their own, having little stake left in the organisation after the decision to leave.*

- *Deciding who is appropriate to interview the leaving person may be difficult. Somebody one level above their direct line manager would be good if the organisation has sufficient levels in the hierarchy.*
- *Deciding what to do with the information received might be tricky as well. If the employee wishes to make a complaint of a personal or confidential nature, it should be pointed out that the manager either has to take it as a formal grievance or not hear it at all. The interview is not a chance to offload grievances without taking responsibility for launching them.*
- *The purpose and aim of the interview needs explaining.*
- *Some employees might find this an intimidating experience and may not respond well. The interviewers will need to be listening rather than questioning, and low key.*

ACTION Carmel decides to discuss the issue at the managers' meeting. The manager concerned expresses some anxieties about having one of her workers interviewed about the manager's style without her there to defend herself. Carmel reassures her that any issues that come up will be raised sensitively with managers and be used as a learning opportunity, not a case for reprimands.

She reminds managers that they have a responsibility to the project to manage staff and to run it as well as possible. Part of that is about staff motivation and keeping staff for a reasonable length of time so that recruitment costs don't get out of hand. In this post there is a high turnover, so an exit interview might reveal issues where managers haven't heard the workers' point of view, for whatever reason.

OUTCOME Carmel interviews the staff member herself and goes through the list of questions:

- Reasons for leaving
- Training needs — were they met?
- Structure of the organisation
- Working relationships and support available
- Management issues
- Salary
- Job satisfaction, effectiveness etc.

She discovers that the work has been divided up in the project so that workers have a regular routine, but little variety in their work since there is a very low client turnover in the eldercare project. It is easy for workers to get bored and demotivated. She decides that this is very useful information and takes it back to the manager.

Carmel overcame her natural reluctance about exit interviews and **COMMENT**
looked at the issue sensitively from the point of view of the
organisation's well-being rather than of the staff or managers. She has
accepted that they work for RESCROFT, and has set up a system that
has a good chance of improving the personnel information and a
channel for structured feedback about the projects.

TIPS ON EXIT INTERVIEWS

- Exit interviews can be revealing about the structure and management of projects.
- They need careful structuring and dealing with to avoid abuse of the opportunity.
- Ideally, it is better if they are carried out by someone above the employee's line manager.
- Tale telling or the breaking of normal rules of management supervision must not be allowed.
- Such interviews are best used as part of a personnel procedures package incorporating supervision, appraisal and exit interviews. This package ensures that there are both standards and safeguards for managers and staff in the management relationship.

[See the sample *Exit Interview Form* in the appendices.]

Carmel introduces a policy on exit interviews throughout the **NEXT STEP**
organisation so that staff and managers know what to expect of
them and feel less anxious about them being carried out. She
encourages managers to feel positive about feedback from their
staff and perhaps introduce a more formal appraisal system that
would spot any problems earlier on in the life of a management
relationship rather than after several months of unhappy working.

3 MANAGEMENT COMMITTEE AGREEMENT TO RECRUIT

Who and when should you consult about staffing levels and recruitment issues?

Sian is writing her annual work plan for the National Organisation of Health Promotion (NOHP). She wants to press on with recruitment plans for a new team of health promotion specialists developing projects working with young people. This was agreed in the long-term plan at the last organisational review day. However, Sian and the treasurer of the Management Committee are at loggerheads over the timing of the recruitment.

The treasurer will not agree to the workers being recruited until the money is in the bank account. This may well result in a delay of three months to the start of the project, and consequently three months less service. Sian wants to go ahead once the contract has been signed with the funders.

There is another issue about the new team of workers. If they are recruited, they will all be on fixed-term contracts and will have to have different and less favourable terms and conditions of employment than the rest of the staff. For example, the permanent contract offers good maternity leave provisions after one year's service. The fixed-term contract will have to offer the statutory provision. This is partly because the level of funding agreed would not cover a percentage for the reserves in case workers wanted to take up these options. Sian wanted to say the NOHP could use its own reserves, but the treasurer was adamant that this would not happen for the fixed-term contract workers.

Sian has a further pressure of having received two very good CVs out of the blue from people who would make excellent health promotion specialists and who have the relevant skills and applications. She doesn't want to lose the opportunity to encourage these people to apply for the up-coming posts.

Should Sian: OPTIONS

- go ahead with the recruitment and risk alienating the treasurer?
- discuss the recruitment timing at the next Management Committee meeting?
- have an emergency meeting with the chair of the Management Committee and the treasurer to come to an executive decision about the issue?

Accepting funding for particular time-limited projects always carries **ISSUES**
several potential risks:

- *The money may not arrive when the funders said it would.*
- *Recruitment has to be delayed.*
- *Contractual terms and conditions are different from those for permanent staff because of funding, which leads to resentments and a two-tier hierarchy of conditions.*

*There may be pressure to try to continue the funding of a successful project at the end of the present funding term. Unfortunately this leads to uncertainty for staff whose contracts might or might not be renewed, and there are legal difficulties with extending fixed-term contracts. [See **Scenario 5: Fixed-Term Contracts**.]*

Accepting CVs that arrive on the desk and carrying out some sort of preliminary screening is not an acceptable equal opportunities practice. Applicants who send CVs should all be sent a letter explaining organisational policy on recruitment through application forms, giving a list of up-coming recruitment if you know what that is likely to be, and advising them where to look out for your adverts in the press.

Sian has to accept that the Management Committee will not allow   **OUTCOME**
her to recruit when she wants to for these posts. She feels angry
and upset and thinks that they are a bunch of fuddy-duddies who
have no idea how to run a modern charity. She is also angry with
the funders for not being clear about when the money was going to
come through and in creating this delay.

Unfortunately smaller charities with small reserves are often in **COMMENT**
*difficult positions regarding recruitment. However, the Management
Committee are absolutely right not to let her spend the money on
recruitment before they have firm guarantees about exactly how
much and when the money will arrive. Funders are notorious for not
announcing awards until later than they said they would and for not
producing money on time.*

TIPS ON PLANNING RECRUITMENT

- Make sure that you allow enough time between putting in an application for funding and the desired start of the project to allow for recruitment.

- Do not start recruitment without the money in the bank or a signed contract.

- Try to give as favourable terms and conditions of work as possible to avoid a two-tier approach to core workers and temporary or project workers developing.

- Don't give preferential treatment to people who send in CVs, however good they may look on paper.

NEXT STEP Sian re-thinks the timing of the project and continues to plan the recruitment for the health promotion specialists, but delays the adverts going to press.

4 JOBSHARE / PART-TIME WORKING

Handling a request for jobsharing or part-time work

Adam manages Alcohol Counselling Service. He has just had a letter from the Administrator, Judy, who has been on maternity leave. She is informing him of her wish to return to work, but on a jobsharing or part-time basis. Her job is a pivotal one in the office. She manages the shop front office, acts as a receptionist and knows everything about the project. Adam has missed her efficiency while she has been on leave. In theory Adam feels sympathetic to her request, but it feels like an additional burden placed on his shoulders when he was hoping to get her back full-time.

Should Adam: OPTIONS

- check the contract of employment to see what it says?
- check the legal position and check with the Management Committee chair, since employing a jobshare would cost more?
- write back and say no outright?

- *There is no automatic right to return to work on a jobshare basis or* **ISSUES** *to be allowed to jobshare (but it may be indirectly discriminatory to refuse) or to work part-time whether or not you have been on maternity leave [see **Legal information** at the end of this section].*
- *Jobsharing generally benefits both workers and organisations owing to increased flexibility and two heads for the price of one.*
- *Introducing jobsharing is an easy way to be more 'family friendly' to all employees, male or female.*
- *If you are going to go down this route, a proper policy about application, recruitment, selection, appointment and careful management practices must be worked out.*
- *There are some additional costs of jobsharing: two lots of national insurance and health insurance (if you have any); training staff. However, most employers find that any additional costs are outweighed by the benefits of higher productivity, lower absenteeism and reduction in staff turnover.*

PLANNING Adam consults the contract and finds that it gives Judy a right to request to return on a jobshare basis if 'the conditions are suitable.' He looks at the legal position and sees that it might be indirectly discriminatory to refuse her request to return to a part-time job — the rules about how to decide depend upon each organisation's situation. He also discusses the issue with the local Council for Voluntary Service (CVS) employment unit.

ACTION Adam reckons up how much it would cost to offer a jobshare and consults with the chair of the Management Committee. They decide that it would be more beneficial to the organisation to split the job into two different part-time posts of secretary/receptionist and administrator/office manager, rather than offering a jobshared administrator post. This fits in with the organisational plan of small growth and an increasing need for more administration time to free up Adam to do more fundraising.

OUTCOME Judy is offered an option to return to either a three-day secretarial/receptionist or an administrator/office manager post on a raised salary grade with additional training to fill in her gaps in skills. Judy accepts the latter. Adam does a full job analysis for both posts and begins recruitment for a secretary/receptionist.

COMMENT *This is a convenient solution that fitted neatly into the organisation plan. The real dilemmas occur when it doesn't and the organisation feels it is making more of an accommodation to women returners than it wants to, perhaps out of the fear of being taken to a tribunal. The option to institute more flexible working should always be seriously considered as it is a positive employment practice, but balanced against the additional costs of employment, managing another person and integrating them into a team.*

TIPS ON JOBSHARING OR PART-TIME WORK

- Take all requests seriously, don't dismiss them out of hand.
- Take legal advice where you are not sure if the indirect discrimination charge might apply to you.
- Be positive but balanced about requests for jobsharing or part-time working. The needs of the project come first, but where it all fits in, the outcome can be highly satisfactory.
- Be aware of additional management responsibilities once there are more people on the staff.
- Men have no legal right to jobshare at all.

Adam makes sure he knows what is in the contract and what the **NEXT STEP**
rights of women returners and part-timers are.

Returning to work after 14 weeks leave. The woman has the right to **LEGAL**
come back to the same job she left and does not have to give notice **ASPECTS**
of her intention to return unless she plans to come back earlier than **OF JOB**
the 14 weeks period. **SHARING /**

Returning after 40 weeks leave. A woman must respond positively to a **PART-TIME**
letter from her employer which is normally sent not earlier than 21 **WORK**
days before the end of the maternity leave period about her
intention to return to work at the end of 29 weeks after the birth.
Failure to reply removes her rights. She must also give 21 days
notice of her intention to return. The job which the woman left
should normally be the one to which she returns, but where this is
not reasonably practicable, then an alternative job can be offered as
long at it is suitable and appropriate and under no less favourable
terms and conditions.

A woman has no automatic right to return to part-time working if
she was full-time before going on maternity leave. However, if the
employers refuse to consider it, they may be acting in an indirectly
discriminatory manner. This is because the imposition of working
full-time may be to the detriment of those who can work only
part-time, mainly women. Indirect discrimination is not
automatically unfair, but the employer would have to show that the
requirement for full-time work was a real need of the organisation,
and must be appropriate to achieve that end. In deciding whether
or not the indirect discrimination is unfair in any particular case
tribunals will look at the size of organisation, the type of staff
employed, how the work is organised, the employment of other
part-time staff and categories of jobs.

Failure to allow a return to work. If an employer refuses to allow a
woman to return to work after taking maternity leave, this will in
most cases be regarded as dismissal and the employee will be able
to make a claim to an industrial tribunal. She is unlikely to succeed
in the claim if:

A) her employer employees five or fewer people and it is not
   reasonably practicable to take her back, and/or

B) she has been offered suitable alternative employment and
   unreasonably refused it.

5 FIXED-TERM CONTRACTS

To offer a permanent contract or a fixed-term one?

The National Organisation of Health Promotion (NOHP) is expanding: Sian has managed to get additional funds through the Single Regeneration Budget (SRB) for three staff for a new project to develop health initiatives aimed at teenagers. She wants to get people into post as soon as possible and is debating what sort of contract to offer them.

OPTIONS Should Sian:

- put them all on permanent contracts, hoping to be able to get further funding after the end of the two years?
- put them on fixed-term two-year contracts, dubious that she could get renewed funding for all three posts?
- employ them as consultants to the organisation?

ISSUES
- *Fixed-term contracts are valuable for short-term projects since staff can be employed for the length of the project only.*
- *A fixed-term contract runs for both parties till the expiry date. This means that termination of the contract before the expiry of the fixed-term may be difficult because the employee may be able to claim unfair or wrongful dismissal. See below under legal information.*
- *A fixed-term contract can be inflexible since it is difficult to vary the terms during the period covered.*
- *There can be legal complexities in drawing up and re-negotiating the contract.*
- *Long-term career development and motivation can be affected as non-renewal of the contract can give rise to feelings of insecurity.*

PLANNING Sian looks into the legal issues of fixed-term contracts and employing consultants. She prepares a paper for the Management Committee and discusses the pros and cons at their next meeting. She plans a recruitment strategy and gets jobs descriptions worked out.

Sian and the Management Committee decide that they will offer **OUTCOME** fixed-term contracts to all the new project workers for three reasons:

- Realistically it is unlikely that they will get renewed funding at a level that they have had from the SRB.
- They want to be clear that any future work under the health promotion initiative will be of a different nature, so as not to lead to dilemmas about which worker to keep on at the end of the contract.
- They realise there are management disadvantages to having some staff on different contracts from each other, but they want to be clear that this project is short-term and peripheral to the core work.

Sian has realistically assessed the prospects for the project and acted **COMMENT** *to try and get the best terms for the employer. She must be careful when recruiting to make sure that workers know there is no likelihood of their contracts being renewed.*

TIPS ON FIXED TERM CONTRACTS

- Always think carefully about the impact of having workers on different terms and conditions of employment — this can be bad for morale.
- Always include a notice period in a fixed-term contract. Otherwise you could be legally obliged to employ the worker until the end of the fixed-term whether you want to or not.
- It is bad practice to issue a fixed-term contract purely as a tactic to avoid paying for possible redundancy. You are then jeopardising workers' rights and commitment to the project for a relatively small cost.
- The current statutory maximum redundancy payment for workers aged between 22 and 41 is £210 per year of service (up to a maximum of 20 years). Anyone who has less than two years' service gets no statutory redundancy money.

Sian draws up a contract for the fixed-term workers.   **NEXT STEP**

LEGAL ASPECTS OF FIXED-TERM CONTRACTS

The legal definition of a fixed-term contract is a contract which it is agreed between the parties will terminate at some future date without notice being given by any party.

A fixed-term contract may be for any period, but to be called fixed-term it must have a termination date. If the termination date passes without any change occurring (i.e. the employee continues working and the employer continues to pay in accordance with the contractual terms) there may come into existence a contract for an indefinite period (by implication), which may be terminable on reasonable notice in the absence of agreement.

If it is intended to rely on the expiration of a fixed-term to terminate the contract, the employee should not be permitted to work on, except on expressly agreed terms, which it is advisable to put in writing.

The expiration of a fixed-term contract without being renewed amounts to a dismissal for the purposes of the 1978 Employment Protection Act.

Notice periods

A fixed-term contract may still be fixed-term even if either party has the ability to end the contract before the declared termination date. To include a notice period allows an employer to sack someone legitimately before the expiry date in the case of poor performance and will allow the employee to resign. The notice period on either side must not be less than the statutory minimum.

There is no notice provision included then it may be assumed that there is a guarantee of employment for the expressed period. However, this will not stand in the way of dismissal for gross misconduct or constructive dismissal.

Waiver clauses

If the fixed-term is for one year or more, the project should include a clause whereby the postholder waives their right to claim unfair dismissal on grounds of the termination of the contract.

If the fixed-term is for two years or more, the project should include a clause waiving the postholder's rights to unfair dismissal on termination of the contract and to redundancy payments on the termination of the fixed-term.

continued overleaf

These waiver clauses are only effective when the contract comes to an end at the stated expiry date. If you dismiss your employee before the end of the contract, the employee may still be entitled to bring a claim for unfair dismissal despite the waiver clause. In this case it would be up to the employer to prove that it was a fair dismissal.

The waiver clauses only apply to the expiry of the contract on the date specified. If the employer terminates the contract before then, the employee has whatever rights their continuous service allows them.

A contract for *one month or less for eight hours or more per week*, where this actually results in employment of three months or more, is treated as a contract of indefinite duration.

A contract for *less than one year* can contain no exclusion clauses, but if such a contract is renewed to last up to two years there may eventually be sufficient continuity of employment for the employee to make a claim for unfair dismissal or redundancy.

6 SESSIONAL STAFF

Casual or sessional workers' rights

Adam is reviewing the use of sessional counsellors at the Alcohol Counselling Service (ACS). ACS currently employs five counsellors to do seven hours per week each at different times of day, so that they can provide a regular service over the phone at advertised times, morning, afternoon and evening as well as back-up face-to-face services to individuals at the office. Adam wants to extend the phone service to five mornings rather than the three currently offered, and the hours available for face-to-face work so that the waiting lists can be cut. He has a grant from the health authority to do this, but they are concerned about equal opportunities in employment and whether the sessional staff are getting good terms and conditions.

OPTIONS **Should Adam:**

- review the sessional contracts counsellors currently have in light of equal opportunities considerations?
- extend the hours of the counsellors who are available to do more work and put them on the permanent staff register?

ISSUES
- *Whatever you call these counsellors — sessional, locum, casual or regular casual — there are still a maze of employment law considerations to think about, which should not be ignored hoping they will go away. [See below under **Legal information**.]*
- *The nature of the contract is different for self-employed and non self-employed people.*
- *You cannot necessarily choose to treat yourself as self-employed.*
- *If someone works a regular number of hours a week on your premises and at times that you dictate, it may be illegal to treat that person as self-employed.*
- *Employees should always be on a contract, regardless of the hours they work, although you do not have to offer them a contract until they get up to eight hours per week.*

24

Adam checks in his legal handbook on good practice for sessional **PLANNING**
staff, then checks the terms and conditions that apply to the current
staff. He finds that he has inherited several different arrangements
from the previous manager.

- Two are treated as self-employed by ACS, but have regular paid
  part-time jobs in other organisations. They do have 'Schedule D'
  (i.e. self-employed) tax numbers.

- One is a genuinely self-employed peripatetic counsellor working
  privately and occasionally as a specialist counsellor on sexual
  abuse cases with a variety of organisations.

- One is on secondment seven hours per week from the local
  education department to run a special group with young people.

- One has a casual contract drawn up in 1987 for two weeks work
  and has been working seven hours per week ever since and
  volunteers in other organisations.

Adam nearly faints at the thought of sorting out this tangle. He **ACTION**
decides that everyone needs to be on as near the same arrangement
as possible. He realises that to unscramble the ones who have been
treated as self-employed will be complex and he decides to consult
the accountant and the local tax office. He gets leaflet IR56 about
the status of self-employed workers and decides that actually they
should be treated as employed because:

- ACS decides when and where they work.
- they use the ACS office and equipment.
- they are being paid whether the phone rings or not.
- they do not provide invoices for the work they are doing.
- they do not offer a rate for performing the job.
- they do not have other clients as self-employed people (they
  are not in business with anyone else).

The secondee presents his own management difficulties [see
Scenario 8: Secondees] but on paper the contract is fine. The final
case annoys him because the worker would have been eligible for
employment rights under the old five year rule if they had been
working for eight hours per week or more.

Adam decides to move everyone except the secondee and the **OUTCOME**
genuinely self-employed person to contracts of employment for a
minimum of eight hours a week and consults the workers about
what their preferences are and how they could do the extra hours.

He has a special meeting with the two workers who should have
been treated as employed, and explains why he is having to change
their status.

COMMENT *Adam has inherited a tangle and has done his best to unravel it. However, if you employ staff they should be given the best legal minimum position. Even if potential staff can provide you with a Schedule D tax number they are not necessarily to be counted as genuinely self-employed.*

TIPS ON EMPLOYING SESSIONAL STAFF

- Review your sessional contracts: are they legal and fair?
- Are your self-employed sessional workers really self-employed? Whether they can produce a schedule D tax reference is the first basic test you need to be worried about, but not the only one. Consult your accountant and/or tax office.

NEXT STEP Adam issues new contracts for all the sessional staff.

LEGAL ASPECTS OF SESSIONAL STAFF

Casual contracts

These are the contracts that usually apply to sessional staff. They are contracts for staff who are employed only when there is work available for them. They are paid for the hours that they work and do not assume any other employee rights.

Continuous employment rights still accrue if casual contracts back onto one another. However, a break in employment of seven days from Sunday to Saturday is enough to break the continuity of accrual of employment rights. This could be as a result either of not being taken on by the employer owing to there being no work, or of the employee not being available for work during that period.

Casual contracts may be indefinite, for a fixed-term or for a particular task. They may be part time: they are temporary contracts as far as the EC Directives are concerned.

It is important to make clear at the outset:

- the basis on which the person is employed.
- the anticipated length of employment.
- what rights will accrue if employment continues.

continued

Payment

- Where a contract of employment is deemed to be entered into, then the project must pay tax and National Insurance for the employee.
- Staff can be treated as self-employed only if they genuinely are, although this can be difficult to define. Always consult your tax office/accountant before treating any staff as self-employed.
- If staff are not self-employed, and you are not their main employer, then you have to deduct tax with no personal allowance, and if they earn more than the NI threshold (£58 per week as at February 1996) then you have to deduct National Insurance as well.
- If the hours of work vary and in some weeks there is no work, then this will jeopardise access to continuity of employment, i.e. accrual of the requisite length of service to claim extra contractual rights.
- If workers fall under the NI earnings threshold they can sign a P46, which means that even if they are self-employed for all their other work, they can be employed for one small piece of work.
- Each tax office can adjudicate only on workplaces in its own area.
- You may get into trouble for back tax and NI contributions if you knowingly collude with illegal payment. Put people who should be onto PAYE straight away and own up. The tax authorities are more likely to treat you leniently if they think you have made a genuine mistake.

MODEL POLICY ON TEMPORARY SESSIONAL WORKERS

- All requests for sessional and temporary staff should normally be authorised by the manager or her deputy.

- Managers should build up a resource book of approved people to contact when needed. If no-one is available from that list, then they should contact a list of approved agencies.

- All temporary sessional workers except agency workers will be required to fill in an application form giving details of experience, abilities, past employment, and two work references. They will also be required to complete a form for police checks (if necessary for the sort of work they do). They will then attend a short interview to assess their suitability. This should be carried out by the manager and the relevant team leader.

- When approved, temporary sessional workers should fill in a standard form which asks for details of salary payments and key personnel details.

- The manager will issue all temporary sessional workers with a contract clearly stating the terms under which they are employed. Where people are contracted on an 'as and when' basis, they will be issued with the sessional contract. Where people are being contracted for a longer period of time, they will be issued with a short-term contract and will be paid on a weekly basis unless contracted for over three months, in which case they will be paid on a monthly basis.

- It is the team leader's responsibility to induct all temporary workers into the policies and practices of the Project and the equal opportunities policy.

7 CONSULTANTS

Using consultants regularly

Sian at the National Organisation of Health Promotion (NOHP) has been using a bank of consultants as researchers and advisers on the development of new health action groups around the country. They are based in five regions and work as required when suitable contracts come along. They are all self-employed and also do work for other clients unconnected with NOHP. They have to come to an induction day on which they are briefed in the NOHP way of working and introduced to the standard sets of materials they are expected to work with. There is no guarantee of work being provided for them and they do not have to take up any work that is offered to them, although if they didn't, then they would probably lose their favoured status quickly. One of the Management Committee members has queried whether working with people like this can really be called 'consultancy' — or if they are actually employees.

Should Sian: **OPTIONS**

- ignore the issue?
- change a system that works for her because of a fear that her office is acting illegally?
- find out more about the difference between an employee and a consultant?

- *Any employee working for an organisation in return for*   **ISSUES**
  remuneration has a contractual relationship with the organisation. There is a distinction between a contract for services and a contract of employment; the latter is sometimes called a 'contract of service'.
- *Just because you call a worker a consultant, it doesn't automatically mean that the Inland Revenue may not judge them to be an employee.*
- *For a contract of employment to exist the individual has to be employed by the organisation and carry out work that is integral to the business.*

- *A contract for services exists when the services are carried out by people who are not an integral part of the business, and who can be deemed to be in business themselves.*
- *Employers are obliged by law to make statutory deductions such as National Insurance for employees who are entitled to statutory employment rights, but not for self-employed workers.*

ACTION Sian gets hold of leaflet IR56 from the tax office and goes through it with the accountant. She checks up on the amount of work that has been passed out to the consultants over the past year and the current status of their businesses.

Sian goes through the main criteria laid down by the courts on whether an engaged person is an employee or not.

- 'Is the person who is engaged to perform the services performing them as a person in business on their own account?'
  — Yes = the contract is for services (independent contractor).
  — No = the contract is of employment and the person is an employee.

- Other relevant considerations in determining this question include:
  — Do the engaged persons hire their own helpers?
  — Do they send in their own invoices?
  — Can they choose their own hours?
  — Do they use their own equipment?
  If the answer to the above is YES, then they are self-employed.

- If you can answer YES to the questions below, then the persons are employees:
  — Are the engaged persons under the total control of the person to whom they are supplying the services? (Who controls when, where and how the work should be done?)
  — Are they obliged to do the work they are given?
  — Is the company obliged to give them work to do?
  — Is it necessary to do the work regularly and possibly within a certain time?
  — Do the persons work under the direction of the Company's management?
  — Has the relationship between the parties endured for a substantial time?
  — Does the company provide the tools and equipment necessary to do the work?

Some of these last points can seem ambiguous. The main point is that you should know if the person you are using is self-employed or not. If they cannot provide you with a Schedule D tax reference then they are not self-employed and you must deduct tax and national insurance contributions for them. Even if they can provide a Schedule D tax reference this may not be enough for them to be treated as genuinely self-employed in relation to your organisation.

If there is genuine doubt, it may be possible to agree that a particular person is self-employed and for that agreement to prevail. If in doubt, check with a lawyer. Use your solicitor, CAB or advice centre to advise you of an employment law specialist.

OUTCOME Sian goes through the checklist and decides that on balance the consultants are self-employed since they can refuse work and can carry it out at their own time and pace even though they have to answer for quality to the Management Committee.

COMMENT *When you use people as consultants on one-off short-term contracts it is easy to distinguish them as self-employed people. You can take people as employees on longer temporary contracts if you want them to be part of the organisation and participate in aspects of the work outside their special role, such as staff meetings.*

When you employ people for regular amounts of work over a long period as self-employed consultants it is more difficult to be clear about the legality of the relationship. These contracts are by no means always clear-cut.

TIPS ON USING CONSULTANTS

- Always be clear about the nature of the work you are taking an employee on to do.
- And be clear about the nature of the contract you are making with them.
- If you get it wrong and pay someone as self-employed when they should be on the payroll, you could be in big trouble with the Inland Revenue.
- A self-employed person will have a Schedule D tax number, which they will be able to show you. (But each case still has to be checked against the criteria.)
- It is possible to have a long-term relationship with a consultant, provided they meet the test requirements each time you use them.

NEXT STEP   Sian checks her assumptions with the status inspector at the local
tax office.

**LEGAL
ASPECTS
OF USING
CONSULT-
ANTS**

- Where you are genuinely employing a consultant, it is good
practice to draw up a contract for services with them.

- The organisation does not pay National Insurance contributions,
pensions schemes, sickness pay, maternity pay, or redundancy
pay. There are no issues about rights of the employee towards
the employer or vice versa.

- The contract should state what is required in the areas below.
(We assume this is a contract which specifies a piece of work,
making recommendations or stating a date for delivery.) Adapt
as necessary depending on which type of consultant you are
using.

   — What service or activity the consultant will carry out: be
     very specific.
   — How the work will be carried out and what access to
     different parts of the organisation the consultant will need.
   — How they should collect information and what the
     boundaries to that information collection are.
   — Confidentiality.
   — Reporting arrangements to whom and how often.
   — Action by the client to ensure success.
   — How the recommendations will be reported.
   — Any consultation on draft reports.
   — Whether there will be any follow-up after the first period of
     consultancy.
   — What is the timescale for the assignment.
   — How much it will cost the organisation in direct costs and
     fees, and any expenses.
   — How often the consultant can bill you and invoicing
     arrangements if the contract is a long one.
   — The effect of illness on schedule and costs.
   — Variations permissible to the contract.

8 SECONDEES

Making the best of a secondment post

The National Organisation of Health Promotion (NOHP) has been offered a secondee from the local Training and Enterprise Council (TEC) who provide some funding for the organisation. Sian had suggested initially that they jointly funded a promotions and publicity post with money from national fundraising. Sian feels anxious about the idea of the secondment on several grounds. Firstly the TEC have a person in mind who is very business-orientated in his thinking and Sian is not sure how relevant his approach would be to NOHP.

Secondly she is dubious about the management position of the secondee. She has heard of projects getting into deep trouble where the arrangement was made informally and there was no clear party who was able to carry out a disciplinary action with the secondee. Thirdly, her personal view is that it would be better to advertise for a person on a fixed-term contract to do this as a discrete piece of work, so that the organisation could set a clear person specification and job description, have a clear employment relationship with the worker and follow equal opportunities recruitment and employment practices.

Should Sian:

OPTIONS

- tell the TEC thanks, but no thanks?
- discuss in more detail why they want to offer her the secondment, what the details of the work and working relationship would be, etc?
- talk to the chair of the Management Committee about the issue and discuss the parameters of what they are willing to accept as a deal?

ISSUES

- *Secondees are an increasingly popular way of gaining skills and extra expertise within the voluntary sector at no direct costs.*
- *A common source of secondees is an arrangement with the local authority, where they support the project and insist on seconded workers or offer secondees in lieu of funding a particular post.*

> • *It is vital to be crystal clear about the management relationship you are entering into. What is happening to the secondee's original contract of employment? In the worst case scenario, can the receiving organisation discipline the secondee?*

PLANNING Sian does not turn down the offer outright, but she clarifies with the chair what they are prepared to compromise on and what not:

- NOHP set the aims and objectives of the work.
- NOHP have a clear employment and management function with the secondee so that they would be able to carry out disciplinary action if the issue arose.
- NOHP draw up a person specification for the work and if the potential secondee meets it they are prepared to take them on; if not they would prefer to advertise.

ACTION Sian sets up a meeting and has a frank discussion with the manager at the TEC about why they have offered the secondment. She goes over her reservations and bottom line position. The TEC offered a secondee because they think that they have a person with good skills to offer, he has a background in a similar field of work and would be interested in working with the NOHP for a short period, they think up to six months.

The TEC manager seems a bit taken aback by Sian's worries about the arrangement. She points out that if it worked well it would be fine, but that problems would arise where it did not work well. Also this person may be able to offer suitable skills but are they the best person for the job? What about the person specification she has drawn up? Does the proposed person meet all the criteria? Will they operate as a full part of the staff team, do they participate in the same way over other decisions or are they apart from the staff group except when discussing their promotions ideas? Who would be managing them; for regular supervision of the project work; for appraisals; for discipline and grievance issues — if they arose?

OUTCOME After consultation with the chair, Sian decides that a secondee is not what she wants, because of possible management difficulties.

COMMENT *Secondments can work, but they can also turn into the most frightful millstones because of lack of clarity about the secondee's role and employment relationship.*

TIPS ON SECONDEES

- Work out what you want from a post first and whether a secondment would be appropriate.

- Don't just accept a secondment because it suits the organisation providing the secondee or funding.

- Insist always on drawing up a secondment document that lays out what is to happen about supervision, management and discipline and grievance issues.

If you are seriously considering a secondment, there are certain arrangements you need to put into your contract. Be sure you make it clear whether the secondment is a temporary job move with the original employer remaining the employer, or whether the new employer is taking over their contract.

LEGAL ASPECTS OF USING SECONDEES

ACTION is an organisation which was formed in 1994 and brings together Action Resource Centre (ARC) and Employees in the Community Campaign. It provides a brokerage service for secondments. It will give advice to voluntary organisations to package their needs into projects, and by working with local and national companies it aims to draw on a wide range of help to support voluntary activity. It sets out to provide a service nationally, but some areas are better served by local offices than others. If there is no local office, ACTION will still give advice to a project on employee community involvement.

FURTHER INFOR-MATION

The head office of ACTION is at 8 Stratton Street, London, W1X 5FD *Tel:* 0171 629 2209.

9 POSITIVE ACTION

Targeting an appointment by using a Genuine Occupational Qualification

Carmel is thinking about the appointment of a new deputy manager for one of the RESCROFT projects in an area with a high proportion of African-Caribbean people. The project has a 60% occupancy rate of African-Caribbeans, but only one member of staff out of ten of that racial origin. Carmel feels that the post would be best filled by someone from that community who could not only provide better direct personal services to the residents, but would advise the rest of the staff on their relationships with the clients and their families if necessary. She is not sure of the actual wording of the law, and is worried in case she might be doing something that is perceived as either illegal or patronising.

OPTIONS Should Carmel:

- consult the Commission for Racial Equality? (CRE)
- consult the chair of the Management Committee?
- go ahead and take the action anyway as she is pretty sure that it complies with the law?

ISSUES *There are several possible positive action measures to take under UK law. The Sex Discrimination Act and Race Relations Act aimed to:*

- *recognise and develop potential that has not been used because of past discrimination and disadvantage.*
- *encourage applications from suitable black and ethnic minority people and women so that they can be considered equally with other candidates.*
- *provide training for black and ethnic minority people and women so that they can become equally qualified with other candidates.*

Each Act has a section that covers the situations where you are specifically allowed to advertise either for a woman or man or a person from a particular racial group. This is called a Genuine Occupational Qualification. When these exemptions are used they must be quoted in the text of the advertisement.

Positive action is NOT:

- *selecting a black or ethnic minority person or a woman irrespective of merit to give an organisation a good image;*
- *selecting a person simply because they are black or from an ethnic minority to create a racial balance;*
- *selecting a woman simply because she is a woman to achieve a balance of the sexes.*

Carmel rings up the CRE and checks under what circumstances she **PLANNING** is allowed to target a post for positive action. She discusses the possibility with the team leader and gets her comments on the idea. Then she informs the chair of the Management Committee of the reasons why she thinks that a Genuine Occupational Qualification should be applied to the post. These are that her organisation:

- will be providing direct personal services of advice and care to residents and their families in the eldercare project.
- will be able to train and advise other staff in their relationships with residents from the African-Caribbean community.

Once Carmel has gained the chair's approval she informs the staff **ACTION** team of her decision and the action that will be taken. She draws up a person specification and job description with the team leader that covers a Genuine Occupational Qualification.

TIPS ON POSITIVE ACTION

Positive action in race equality is necessary because:

- Racism in society, in education, in access to housing and employment has resulted in black and ethnic minority people generally being less able to compete equally with the white population.
- Even if selection criteria and appointment procedures were all changed overnight to remove direct and indirect discrimination, it would take many years to redress the effects of this past discrimination.
- Positive action seeks to put black and ethnic minority people onto a fair footing with white people so that they can compete equally for jobs.
- Positive action can: help women acquire the skills they need to enter a wider range of jobs; maximise the potential of women employees; encourage women to seek promotion and contribute fully to the organisation where they work.

COMMENT *When considering taking positive action measures it is important to be genuine in your motives, not to do it in order to look good or generally to balance the team.*

NEXT STEP Carmel prepares for a new member of staff to come into the team and discusses the use of the Genuine Occupational Qualification with the team leader. They prepare an induction pack.

LEGAL ASPECTS OF POSITIVE ACTION The *Race Relations Act 1976* Section 5(2)(d) provides four exemptions. The one which is the most relevant to voluntary organisations allows for individuals to be selected for a job on racial grounds where they will provide those of their racial group with 'personal services promoting their welfare, and those services can most effectively be provided by a person of that racial group'.

The *Sex Discrimination Act 1975* does not apply when being a woman (or a man) is a Genuine Occupational Qualification for the job. The main occupational qualification used in the voluntary sector is under Section 7 (2) (e):

> "because the nature of the establishment, or that part of it within which the work is done, requires the job to be held by a woman because:
> — it is a single sex hospital or other establishment, or part of an establishment for persons requiring special care, supervision or attendance; and
> — those persons are all women (disregarding the exceptional presence of any man) and
> — having regard to the essential nature of the establishment, it is reasonable that the job should be held by a woman."

Taking positive action is not just about using the Genuine Occupational Qualification rule. You can also encourage people from a particular ethnic minority or sex to apply for the work if they have been under-represented in the past twelve months (Section 38 of the Race Relations Act and Section 48 of the Sex Discrimination Act.)

For example, in advertising, a clause might say :

"The Voluntary Action Group wishes to recruit supervisors for its adventure playground and youth club. African-Caribbeans and Asians are under-represented as leaders and supervisors in our team. We therefore particularly welcome applications from suitably qualified people from these racial groups. Race Relations Act Section 38 (1) (b) applies."

10 WRITING A JOB DESCRIPTION

Drawing up an accurate, lasting job description

Adam is recruiting for a new information/researcher at the Alcohol Counselling Service, as Kostas is leaving. He is concerned to be clear about the work that the new postholder should do. Kostas has developed the way he does his job and what he focuses on. And now the work bears little resemblance to the original job description.

Kostas has taken on work that should properly have been a special project: creating a database for the region on alcohol counselling services. He has been running an informal help and advice desk for interested groups in the same county. This partly came about because of his personal interest in the project and expertise in computers. Other parts of the information work have suffered, and Adam is concerned that what goes into the job description should be accurate, but without wanting to lose all the work Kostas has done on the database.

Should Adam   OPTIONS

- write the database work into the job description and decrease the other aspects of information work? While this will benefit the services ACS provides to outside groups it may adversely affect the work of ACS' own advisors.

- go back to the original job description and leave the database work to be carried out by volunteers under the aegis of the new information worker?

- redraft the emphasis of the job description entirely to reflect the new project, but not be dominated by it?

- *Once each job description in the team is right, many other*   **ISSUES**
  management processes and practices fall into place.

- *Job descriptions must be based on the needs of the organisation and its core purpose, or service delivery standards, not on the needs or personal preferences of the individual currently performing the task.*

- *Getting a clear job description is important because it is a key to successful:*
  - *— recruitment and selection.*
  - *— staff appraisal and supervision.*
  - *— induction.*
  - *— staff development.*
  - *— discipline and grievance procedures.*
  - *— restructuring and review.*
  - *— training needs analysis.*
  - *— staff/team relations.*
  - *— job evaluation.*

PLANNING   Adam decides that he has to put the needs of the organisation first, and spends time discussing the work priorities and future work programme with the staff and the Management Committee. Once he feels clear about how the information and research work could develop to meet the needs of the whole organisation he can proceed with the job description and recruitment, and with further organisational planning.

ACTION   Adam is now clear about:
- the aim and purpose of the job.
- the tasks that need doing.
- the relationship to other jobs in the organisation.
- how the new job fits in with organisation's priorities.
- what sort of support the job gets or gives to other staff.

OUTCOME   Adam drafts a new job description using a standard ACS format:
1. Job title
2. Who the job holder is responsible to
3. Who the job holder is responsible for
4. Special conditions attached to the job
5. Date written or updated
6. Date postholder started
7. Job Summary
8. Job responsibilities

COMMENT   *Not many organisations feel they have the luxury to carry out a full job analysis each time they write a job description. However, it can be beneficial to much of the future success of the job. Good written material provides a sound basis for efficient management of services, appraisal/review sessions and supervision sessions for the postholder and their manager. It is the service to the ACS users that matters, not keeping staff happy or allowing them to develop their own areas of interest at the expense of the organisation's priorities.*

TIPS ON WRITING A JOB DESCRIPTION

If boundaries are set clearly and standards properly determined, monitored and evaluated, all workers can benefit from:

- clear understanding of the purpose of their job.
- clear understanding its importance to the organisation.
- its relation to other jobs in their team.
- better supervision.
- firmly-based and less threatening monitoring and evaluation.
- less worker stress.
- less risk of disputes that are costly in time, money and emotional stress.

Adam plans to review the other job descriptions and update them into a standard format after consultation with the staff. **NEXT STEP**

11 DRAFTING A PERSON SPECIFICATION

Sorting out the skills and experience you need

In the National Organisation of Health Promotion (NOHP), the development worker role is about to be split into two jobs, reflecting the increased amount of work being carried out as a result of the new funding.

The workers will take one region of the country each, but carry out the job in the same way to the same brief. The existing worker, Sohalia, has been involved in the consultation about the new post and has agreed to the split of the regions.

Sian is now faced with having to redraft the job descriptions and write a person specification, which wasn't prepared when Sohalia was appointed. She is worried that Sohalia may be offended if the new person specification stresses skills that she is not particularly strong on.

OPTIONS **Should Sian:**

- have a formal meeting with Sohalia and openly discuss her concerns?

- write the person specification anyway and hope that Sohalia is not going to be offended?

- ask her for her comments on what should be in it and then work with those when she draws up the person specification?

ISSUES *The person specification should list the ESSENTIAL worker characteristics necessary to perform the job successfully. These might include items under some or all of the following headings:*

- *Experience*
- *Skills and abilities*
- *Knowledge*
- *Qualifications and education/training*
- *Other requirements, e.g. travelling, driving*
- *Legal requirements.*

Essential criteria define the level that must be met if the job is to be carried out to required standards. Desirable criteria refine the essential criteria and should only be used to help the panel to shortlist if there are a large number of applicants meeting all the essential criteria. They still need to relate to the performance of the job.

Sian decides that she will have a formal meeting with Sohalia, **ACTION** explain the process of consultation, set the boundaries for action and ask her for her comments on a draft person specification but that she, Sian, will have final overall control of the end-product. Sian will also offer training for Sohalia if there are any criteria that come up which she is not as qualified in as the organisation would like.

Sian drafts the person specification, following the process outlined **OUTCOME** below:

1. She goes through the job description, examining each main task or group of tasks and writing a criterion for each area under the headings above.

2. Then she lists all the ones she thinks she might use. She ensures that the criteria are testable/measurable in some way. Sian tries to write them as specifically as possible in detailed sentences. For example, instead of "Proven Management Skills" she puts:
   "2 years experience of directly supervising staff or volunteers in a paid or unpaid capacity.
   2 years experience of planning and prioritising the aims, objectives and regular tasks of an organisation."

3. Sian now goes back over the list and cuts it radically. She is aiming for a maximum of 13 headings: 10 essential and 3 desirable points in the final version.

4. Then Sian prioritises her chosen criteria, deciding if they are essential or desirable.

5. Finally she ensures that she knows how she is going to test for each criterion. Will it be at the shortlisting or interview stage?

Once Sian has a draft she checks it with the Management Committee and consults with Sohalia.

Writing a person specification is one of the most difficult tasks in any **COMMENT** *recruitment process. Always check your draft with another person to see if it reads the way you intended it to.*

TIPS ON DRAFTING A PERSON SPECIFICATION

- The criteria should be written in as specific a way as possible without being intimidating or stereotypically exclusive.

- Factors such as skills and transferable life experience may be given equal weight with formal qualifications. For example, if the job requires organisational and administrative skills, then experience in running a playgroup or involvement in a Parent Teachers Association or community group fundraising can demonstrate those skills.

- Experience gained from voluntary Management Committee work or in another unpaid capacity may demonstrate valid management abilities.

- Do not include qualifications that are over-specific for the job, or take the possession of a degree as being a sign of some ineffable personality trait that is a 'good thing'.

- It may be indirect discrimination to specify qualifications that can be acquired only in the UK, for example CQSW. Put 'CQSW or equivalent.'

- Don't deliberately include criteria that profile a person through personality type. For example:

    'cheerful disposition'

    'must be able to work long hours'

    'must be able to work under stress'

    can be hidden signals for 'only uncomplaining women need apply' or 'only people with no personal commitments outside work need apply'.

NEXT STEP   Sian consults on the draft person specification with Sohalia and the Management Committee; then finalises it and the rest of the job pack.

12 PREPARING AN APPLICATION FORM

Drafting the form that tells you the most about the applicants

Carmel has been inspired to review her recruitment process at RESCROFT after having difficulty in learning enough about the calibre of applicants from the application form. Some of the people shortlisted were OK and some did not seem to meet adequately the criteria being used on the person specification. Carmel realised that this was probably because the application form was an old standard one the organisation had been using since its early days. It was based on one used in her own recruitment, that had been adapted by the Management Committee from a local authority example. Carmel is pushed for time because there is a recruitment coming up for the new project manager and she doesn't want to delay it.

Should Carmel: OPTIONS

- push on with the recruitment this time, and leave redrafting of the form until she has more time to spare?
- redraft the form anyway given that there is never a right time and she has the added benefit of a time deadline to keep her to the task?
- delegate it to the personnel sub-committee of the Management Committee, and hope they come up with a new draft in time for the recruitment?

- *The purpose of the application form is to see if applicants meet the* ISSUES *criteria on the person specification. It must be able to do this by asking specific questions based on those criteria.*
- *Each application form will need different specific questions as well as some standard features.*
- *It should be easy to fill in, have enough space for clear answers and provide the information needed for shortlisting.*

ACTION Carmel discusses the balance of the available time versus the urgency to get on with the recruitment with the chair of the Management Committee. The chair agrees that the form would be better redrafted and offers to come in and go through it with her one afternoon. As they are both on the personnel sub-committee anyway, they decide this can form a final draft to be approved at the sub-committee meeting next week.

OUTCOME The form they design contains the following points:

Personal details: Name, address and phone number and equal opportunities monitoring questions are put on a front sheet which can be detached from the main body of the form after both have been numbered. This adds to anonymity in shortlisting and is good equal opportunities practice.

Main part of the form: The main part of the form will have questions relating to the skills, experience and abilities needed for the job. Each point in the person specification will be covered with a specific question related to each point.

Access needs: A question on access or applicants' other needs in order to be able to attend the interview.

Past criminal offences: Since the job includes access to people under the age of 18 who are vulnerable, Carmel and her chair decide to ask a question about past criminal convictions. (These should not be asked as a matter of course, but included only when absolutely necessary, following the criteria in the Rehabilitation of Offenders Act. For certain jobs it is essential to ask about previous criminal convictions. For example, for all jobs in places required to be registered under the Registered Homes Act and those providing young people under 18 with accommodation, care, social services or training. For a full list of occupations exempt under the Act consult the Home Office or an up-to-date employment law manual.

References: Space for two referees who can comment on how the person meets the person specification criteria and to ask if they can be contacted before interview or only if you are to offer the applicant the post. [See *Scenario 27* for a more detailed discussion of references.]

COMMENT *Carmel has balanced the time pressures with urgent management needs and has progressed the personnel management expertise within the organisation. This should lead to a better shortlisting process in future.*

TIPS ON PREPARING AN APPLICATION FORM

- Do not include irrelevant questions on the form, for example asking for all educational qualifications since GCSEs when experience gained in other ways is more important.

- Questions should always be as specifically related to the post as possible. On equal opportunities, for instance, if recruiting an advice worker you might ask:

    "What do you think are the key issues in implementing an equal opportunities policy in a neighbourhood advice centre?"

- Ask about people's ability to travel, possession of a driving licence etc, if this is relevant, but do not ask questions like whether they could manage to work unsocial hours or work under pressure. This could lead to discrimination against people with dependents and people with disabilities, and they should be the ones to decide, not you. In the interview, make clear what the hours of work are and ask if they have understood this and can work at those times.

- The layout of the form is important. There should be adequate space for each answer; this gives the applicants a good idea of the importance you attach to each question and the amount you want them to write. The form often ends up four or five sides long.

- If you have to have a standard form then you could adopt a slightly different solution: keep the front page detachable and ask the applicants to fill in the rest of the form taking the person specification points one by one in the order in which they appear in the person specification. Give them an idea of how much space to use.

Carmel draws up the draft with the Chair of the Management Committee and uses it for the current recruitment.   **NEXT STEP**

13 THE ADVERT

Making it attractive and effective

When Adam comes to draft the advert for the new information researcher job at Alcohol Counselling Service (ACS) he realises that he has a harder task than he thought. He wants to include as much information as possible, but in a short space, and as cheaply as possible while still making the advert attractive. He is facing a major set of dilemmas about what to emphasise and what not to. He is also not sure about the job title. Should it be Information Worker, Research Worker, Information and Computer Worker, Information Support Worker?

OPTIONS **Should Adam:**

- go for a very small ad with the logo, job title and salary only?
- draft a longer advert and then cut back to the basics?
- emphasise computer skills at the expense of information skills?

ISSUES
- *The advert must follow from the person specification and job description.*
- *Attracting too many applicants is as bad as getting too few. It wastes a lot of time and money in sending out details to unsuitable people.*
- *It must list the key skills necessary to do the job and give enough information for potential applicants to de-select themselves.*
- *What must be in the advert:*
  - *Organisation's name and logo*
  - *The job title*
  - *Where the job is based*
  - *A good idea of the main duties involved and main aspects of the person specification, and any qualifications required*
  - *The salary (either the amount or the scale if you use a recognised one), and any allowances*
  - *An equal opportunities statement*
  - *The closing date (and interview date)*
  - *Where to get further details*
  - *Registered Charity Number.*

- *Include the following if they apply:*
  - *The duration of the post if it is for a fixed-term*
  - *The hours if it is not full-time*
  - *Jobsharer's statement (If you have a policy on jobsharing)*
  - *A statement of any positive action, encouragement to apply*
  - *A reference to any Genuine Occupational Qualification exemptions you are using under the Race Relations or Sex Discrimination Acts*
- *A double tick symbol is used by the Department of Employment to symbolise commitment to good practice in the employment of people with disabilities. Consult the DOE on when you can use it.*

ACTION

Adam gets Judy, the administrator, to ring round the main publications he wants to get the advert in and find out about deadlines and prices and what artwork they need. He reminds her to ask for a charity discount. He drafts a couple of versions of the job ad and sends it to the Chair of the Management Committee.

OUTCOME

Adam finally settles on the following text for his advert:

INFORMATION OFFICER

to provide an information service to staff of Alcohol Counselling Service and related agencies.

We are looking for someone with 2 years experience of specialist information work. Managing a computer database, writing skills and networking in the voluntary sector essential experience.

Salary Scale 6: Holidays 30 days per year.

For further information and an application form please send an A4 SAE to ACS, Newtown.

Closing date 21/9/95.   Interview date 9/10/95.

ACS works within equal opportunities principles, and is a registered charity.

COMMENT *Adam was aided in his dilemmas because he had already drawn up a clear person specification and job description, so he knew exactly what the main points were that needed to go in the advert. The main difficulty was summarising the information and making the job attractive and eye-catching to get as many well-qualified candidates as possible.*

TIPS ON WRITING ADVERTS

- Don't compromise on text information to save a few pounds. You may leave out too much information and encourage too many people to think they could do the job.
- The text needs to be as eye-catching as possible. Emphasise the main points.

LEGAL ASPECTS OF THE ADVERT If you are using a Genuine Occupational Qualification in the job advert, the relevant section of the law must be stated.

Organisations that have 20 or more paid staff, and where less than 3% of those are people with registered disabilities or the potential to be registered, can take positive action to recruit more people with disabilities. You can legally say in the advert that applications from people with registered/registerable disabilities will be given priority.

Note: The 1996 Disability Discrimination Act will introduce significant changes to the rights of people with disabilities not to be discriminated against, and will introduce new responsibilities and obligations for employers.

14 WHERE TO ADVERTISE

Getting to the best applicants

Sian is anxious to get to the best applicants for the very important development worker expansion post for the National Organisation of Health Promotion. They want to attract a high-calibre person who can join early and start working effectively as soon as possible. Sian wants to carry out NOHP's equal opportunities policy and advertise as widely as possible.

Should Sian: OPTIONS

- go for a main national newspaper and leave it at that?
- put it in the main national newspaper and also a few leading minority ethnic journals, disability papers and specialist press?
- carry out a leafleting exercise as well?

The equal opportunities policy states that advertising should be as **ISSUES** *wide as possible, but does not specify where ads should be placed. Sian does not want to advertise in all the possible places without having a good idea that she will get an appropriate response.*

Sian's budget is £1,400. This gives her some flexibility but she has to balance out costs/equal opportunities considerations and potential effectiveness of the placing for suitable responses.

The advert should be placed where people who meet the person specification are most likely to read it. It might be the mainstream black press, gay press, women's press, or specialist disability press. You can try out particular papers read by any groups you are targeting and use the ones that you get the best results from.

NOHP is a second-tier organisation and needs a development worker who knows about the work of local health promotion units. As NOHP has a database of these health promotion units, it can send out the advert as a leaflet really easily as part of its own regular monthly mailing to these units.

If there were a black workers' or women workers' health promotion network, that would be an appropriate place to advertise.

OUTCOME Sian spends time thinking about the advert and where to place it for best effect. She consults the chair of the Management Committee and then decides that they will advertise in the *Guardian* for two weeks running and the *Voice* for two weeks running, time the adverts to coincide with the monthly *Health Promotion Workers Bulletin,* and leaflet key organisations on their mailing list.

COMMENT *Sian has got the balance right between costs and circulation of the advertisement. She has taken some positive action measures, placing it in the Voice and Guardian. Placing it in the specialist mailing is a good way to get it to people with the right experiences and skills who are already working in the field.*

TIPS ON WHERE TO ADVERTISE

- The following are guidelines for advertising, whether you are considering an executive or an administrative post. Obviously some flexibility may be kept to meet the needs of specific instances.
- The first decision is whether to choose:

  a local trawl — suitable where a good range of applicants will be available locally, e.g. administrative, lower level finance posts. These posts are unlikely to be 'different' enough to encourage mobility from outside the local area.

  a national trawl — where numbers and quality of applicants may be limited by making a local restriction, and/or where the attraction of the job will mean quality candidates will be prepared to be mobile.

- Costs will always be taken into account, which will mean restricting the trawl in some instances. This is likely to be particularly the case with temporary or part-time posts.
- If you're taking positive action or affirmative action measures, then place the advert in the press read by the under-represented community.
- See overleaf for some ideas of specific places to advertise.

Local:

- Local/regional press
- Job centre including Disablement Resettlement Officer
- Local black press where available
- Specialist local disability organisations
- Local radio.

National:

- National press
- National ethnic minority or women's press
- National gay press
- Appropriate trade/professional press to be considered
  e.g. Personnel Management for personnel managers
- Northern Ireland press
- Specialist disability press.

CHECK-LIST FOR PLACING ADVERTS

No advert should be discriminatory or biased in favour of one sex or race directly or indirectly and publications have an obligation to turn adverts down if they think they are discriminatory.

LEGAL ASPECTS OF ADVERTS

15 INTERNAL APPOINTMENTS

Do you need to advertise?

At RESCROFT, the post of deputy manager in one of the teams is going to be advertised under positive action, using a Genuine Occupational Qualification under the Race Relations Act. Carmel has spent a lot of time working on the recruitment package and the job advert and has just presented her materials and plan to the Executive Committee. Now, one of the staff has asked about the possibility of allowing internal applicants first.

Are there any suitably qualified candidates who might be interested in the post? Carmel has to admit that she doesn't know. There are certainly other members of the staff from the African-Caribbean community, some of whom would make good deputy managers. The unwritten policy has always been to advertise to attract as wide a field as possible from which to choose the best applicant. Now Carmel is confused about her options.

OPTIONS **Should Carmel:**

- open the post to internal advertising, making it plain that any internal candidates still have to meet the criteria for the post?
- advertise externally, and encourage suitably qualified internal candidates to apply if they want alongside external candidates?

ISSUES *It is important to weigh up the advantages and disadvantages if you are considering internal appointments. The principles of equal opportunity have to be considered against the benefits of an internal career system and providing opportunities for promotion. Internal appointments can save a lot of money on advertising. On the other hand you should be clear about their disadvantages:*

- *If you have a mainly white workforce at present, you are not going to diversify the workforce if you use internal appointments.*
- *You could be accused of favouritism if you appoint internally.*
- *In a small organisation there are not going to be enough potential candidates to guarantee that you get the best possible person.*
- *You often benefit from the fresh input of an outsider.*

Carmel thinks long and hard about this. She is concerned not to break the principles of equal opportunities and not to be open to even a hint of favouring particular internal candidates. As this option has come up at the last minute, she is anxious about being accused of creating these 'special' opportunities for people from a particular ethnic group whereas other minorities have not had this option before. She does not want the internal person to be afraid that they got the job with fewer skills than a potential outsider.

PLANNING

There are four possible internal applicants who could meet the criteria on the person specification. Carmel decides that this is enough internal competition to make internal applications feasible.

Carmel decides that internal appointments are an option not just for this appointment but for all appointments at deputy and manager level. There could also be opportunities for sideways transfers between projects to gain different experiences.

ACTION

She does not want to rush into this policy, but is wary of further delay on this particular post. However, the potential savings on advertising are huge, so she decides to draft a policy, circulate it to the staff, the Executive Committee and the union representatives in double quick time and see if it can be approved in principle in time for this appointment.

When she begins to draft the policy she sees that it could have many benefits, provided that the organisation continues to recruit a diverse group of people from outside into team member positions and at the higher levels.

One month later at the next Executive Committee meeting, Carmel presents her policy on internal appointments. As RESCROFT now has a total of 40 staff it is felt appropriate for the deputy project manager and project manager jobs to be open to internal appointments. The committee also decides on a policy of allowing transfers between jobs for project workers so that they can gain experience in different projects to enable both career development and job satisfaction.

OUTCOME

Carmel has been realistic about her options and boldly gone for a pragmatic approach. She could have been cautious and waited until the next recruitment package to make sure that she wasn't delaying the recruitment process too much by changing the policies of the organisation half way through. Then she would in fact have delayed the recruitment process.

COMMENT

TIPS ON INTERNAL APPOINTMENTS

- The principle of equal opportunities has to come first when judging whether a system of internal appointments might work.
- They are fair to use once you already have a group of workers who fully represent the local ethnic make-up of the population and other aspects of balance.
- They can offer career development opportunities for existing staff.
- They mean that you can retain experienced staff and increase their effectiveness as managers in a short time because they need less induction.
- You have to be scrupulous in applying the same person specification standards and criteria to internal appointments as you would to external candidates, otherwise you are open to accusations of favouritism.
- If the internal applicant does not get the job, then you can open it to external candidates through the usual methods.
- If there are internal candidates and they don't get the job, then you need to be careful about telling them why and handling any repercussions among the rest of the staff.
- Internal appointments can be a good way of saving money, but should never be used simply for that purpose to compromise the principle of equal opportunities.
- Internal appointments are not feasible in small or very small organisations.

NEXT STEP Carmel discusses the new policy at the team leaders' meeting and points out specific opportunities in recruitments approaching.

16 EQUAL OPPORTUNITIES MONITORING FORM

Checking for bias in the recruitment process

Terry, a new member of the Alcohol Counselling Service Management Committee, has been talking to Adam on the phone about monitoring the recruitment process. He is a local authority officer and is very keen to institute monitoring systems.

Adam can see the point, but Terry has raised this issue just as the recruitment package is being finalised and this means more work for Adam at the last minute. Adam is aware that there are issues about confidentiality and about whether you use forms that are separate from the main body of the application form or not. But he doesn't really know where to go for more information — or how to judge what approach he needs to take.

Should Adam:
OPTIONS

- not bother with a monitoring form this time — it seems complicated and he wants to do it right if at all?
- be confident that his other measures have removed bias: so there is no need?
- use the local authority approach or design one specially?

ISSUES

- *Monitoring a recruitment process is important because it can reveal where discrimination may still be happening.*
- *You can monitor any aspects covered by your equal opportunities policy, for example; race, age, gender, sexuality, level of physical ability (and where applicants saw the advert).*
- *There are three main methods of equal opportunities monitoring in use in the voluntary sector:*
  1. A detachable front page of the application form for personal details and information to be used for monitoring. The front page and the rest of the form are given the same number and the monitoring information is put away until after the shortlisting process is complete. This makes it the most anonymous method of shortlisting, and answering the monitoring questions is virtually compulsory.

2. *The monitoring form is separate from the application form and is returned in a separate envelope, unnumbered. You are relying on applicants returning them voluntarily, and can monitor only applications, not the rest of the process. This is the most anonymous method of all but provides no information about possible bias during the selection process.*

3. *A separate monitoring form is returned with the application, but voluntary. Those returned are numbered, so you can track the process. Personal details still appear on the application form seen by all shortlisters.*

ACTION   Adam does some research on monitoring and checks which form the local CVS and CRE recommend. He discusses with the chair of the Management Committee what can be done this time and how they should improve the system for next time.

OUTCOME   Adam agrees that a monitoring form is useful but that he can't redesign the whole application form at this late stage. It will have to go out as a separate document. Both forms will be given the same number when they are sent out and the covering letter will explain that the monitoring form will not be used as part of the recruitment process. Both forms can be tied up to each stage of the process after the selection is complete.

NEXT STEP   Adam designs a new monitoring form for the recruitment process to summarise the decisions made at each stage, which can be tied in with equal opportunities monitoring results. If there are any anomalies suggested by the results of the equal opportunities monitoring, then the process monitoring forms can be checked through for contributory potential discriminatory actions. Adam redesigns the application form to integrate the monitoring form in time for the next recruitment process.

TIPS ON MONITORING SELECTION

- Monitoring selection processes is recommended by the EOC and CRE codes of practice.
- The EOC and CRE also recommend monitoring the whole recruitment process using a record sheet on which the decisions made at each stage of the recruitment process are summarised and recorded.
- Once you have the data, how can you tell if you are being biased or not? The two main methods of checking your data are described overleaf.

The 4/5ths rule. Several Government Agencies in the USA have **CHECKING** adopted this rule for comparing the relative success rate of **FOR BIAS** different groups. The rule states that "If the selection rate for any race, sex or ethnic group falls below 4/5ths (80%) of the rate for the most successful group, this will be regarded as evidence of adverse impact". In other words something in the recruitment process is leading to discrimination taking place.

Equality Ratio. This is calculated from statistics for the number of black and white applicants and appointees.

For example:

Number of applicants		Number appointed	
white	black	white	black
450	150	10	3

1. Number of black people appointed is divided by the number applying:

$$3/150 = x \quad (0.02)$$

2. Number of white people appointed is divided by the number applying:

$$10/450 = y \quad (0.022)$$

3. Figure for black people is divided by the figure for white people:

$$x/y = z$$

$$0.02/0.022 = 0.909$$

4. If the equality ratio (z) equals 1.00 then there is equality in the experience of black and white people in the process. If it is less than 1.00 then black applicants have fared worse than white applicants.

17 WHAT TO SEND OUT TO APPLICANTS

Telling people enough without being overwhelming

Adam has prepared his recruitment package for the post of Information Officer for Alcohol Counselling Service (ACS) and now has to decide exactly which bits of information need to be sent out to applicants. He has amassed a large stack of potential information for the post and wonders just how much he needs to send out to all applicants and how much can be kept for those shortlisted. He has to send out the following as a bare minimum, and hopes that the photocopier won't break down under the strain as it is:

- A covering letter
- The job description
- The person specification
- A copy of the equal opportunities policy
- An application form

OPTIONS Should Adam:

- not send out anything extra to the above?
- send out an annual report?
- send out a project description but not an annual report?

ISSUES *The number of applicants you are likely to receive for a post depends very much on the type of job, how specialist it is and how popular the work is. It also depends on putting enough information in the advert for people to self-select themselves and self-de-select. There is no point in getting 200 enquirers and 200 applicants for each job. Ideal would be 100 enquirers and 30 high-quality applicants. This can give us a few principles about sending out information:*

- *Send out enough information to allow applicants to choose whether they think they can do the job and whether they would like working for you.*
- *Don't send detailed project information out at the first stage of enquiry, a brief description is enough.*
- *More detailed information can then be sent out to shortlisted candidates, and saves on postage costs.*

Adam decides that he will send out the following information in **ACTION**
addition to the above:

- **Project information** (1 page of A4)
    - The project's overall aims.
    - How the Management Committee and any other committees
      work, what the other staff do.
    - Where the money comes from and how secure funding is.

- **General job information** (2 pages of A4)
    - How the the job fits into the project and organisation.
    - Details of any induction, supervision and support.
    - Details of career opportunities and training available in the
      job.
    - The amount of travelling and overnight stays involved and
      whether caring costs are paid in those circumstances.
    - A description of the accessibility of any buildings the worker
      will be using.
    - Whether the job is open to job-sharers, and under what terms
      and conditions they would be employed.
    - A summary of the main terms and conditions, including the
      salary and scale. (He realises that you can't assume that
      applicants will keep a copy of the advertisement.)

This is quite a substantial amount of information but it is targeted **COMMENT**
specifically at the job applicants and should enable them to self-select
in applying for the job on offer.

TIPS ON WHAT TO SEND TO APPLICANTS

- Once the material has been collated and prepared for
  use in one recruitment package, it can be adapted
  easily for future recruitments.
- Make sure you explain in the covering letter what is
  in the pack, so that applicants know why it is all
  there.
- Materials prepared, or adapted, specifically for each
  job are worth the additional effort, as they enable
  applicants to judge the job and the organisation
  better, and help them to prepare for the interview if
  they are shortlisted.

NEXT STEP Adam drafts the covering letter for enquirers which:

- reminds applicants of the closing date.
- states the interview dates if known.
- tells applicants whether or not receipt of their form will be automatically acknowledged.
- points out the monitoring section at the start of the application form, and gives people full reasons why it is included.
- informs people when they can expect to hear if they are shortlisted and whether they will be told if they are not shortlisted.
- includes details of when he would like the successful applicant to start if there are any particular considerations.

[See *Appendix VII* for a sample covering letter.]

18 SHORTLISTING I

Whom to involve

Sian at the National Organisation of Health Promotion (NOHP) is being heavily lobbied by two different interest groups on the recruitment for the new development worker. Sohalia, the worker whose job is being split, wants to be on the selection panel; she says she will have to work the closest with the new worker and will need to make sure whoever it is fits into the team.

Three of the Management Committee members have said that they are very keen to be involved. Brian, the chair of the committee, says that he should be involved on principle in the recruitment of a key worker post. Jean has very strong ideas about how the development work should be done and wants to make sure that the appointee follows her views, and Barbara represents youth interests on the committee and has concerns about the type of person who will be recruited. She maintains that the new appointee must be young and of an image to fit in with the young people's health projects that they want to recruit to membership.

Should Sian: OPTIONS

- include Sohalia on the panel?
- include all three of the committee members and herself, but no other staff people?
- have a maximum of three, with only one committee representative?

The shortlisting panel should be the same people who follow through **ISSUES**
the whole selection and appointment, so they are an important group of people to get right. There are some issues about the number and skills needed on the panel that will help Sian to decide.

- *Three people on the panel is ideal if they represent all the skills needed. You should never have more than five people on a panel.*
- *Panel members must all be trained in the recruitment process and have equal opportunities interviewing skills.*

- *Members must between them have the specialist knowledge and the ability to measure whether the candidates can meet the person specification criteria.*
- *Ideally the panel should be representative of the committee, senior managers and workers in the relevant team.*
- *The panel should also represent different races and sexes to counteract any potential stereotypical influences.*
- *Any issues about the skills needed to do the job should be sorted out during the design of the job description and person specification, not argued out at shortlisting or interviewing.*

PLANNING Sian decides that she will have to discuss the issue with the chair of the Management Committee. She prepares a checklist of who might be on the panel.

	MC	Trained	Skills	Colour	Axe to grind
Sian	N	Y	Y	White	N
Brian	Y	N	N	Black	N
Barbara	Y	N	Y	White	Y
Jean	Y	Y	Y	Black	Y
Sohalia	N	Y	Y	Black	Y

Sian and Brian look at the list and discuss the issues. They agree that it may be problematic to have both Jean and Barbara on the panel since they both have special interests that they wish to safeguard. Sian wishes that they had raised these matters before in committee so that they could have been sorted out earlier.

ACTION Sian convenes a meeting of potential panel members with Brian and goes through the issues. She discusses openly the nature of representation on the panel and her concerns about the issues overtaking the person specification criteria. She is also concerned about Sohalia basing her judgements on 'gut feelings' about whether the new person would get on with her rather than balancing her skills and being a good team person.

OUTCOME They have an assertive discussion about these points and agree the following. The panel will be Sian (chair), Sohalia and Jean. They are all trained, have the skills necessary to test the candidate and make up a mixed panel. It would have been good to have a man, but Brian is not a specialist in development work and is not trained. Jean and Barbara agree that their concerns are represented in the person specification criteria and Barbara feels confident that Jean will represent her interests on the panel.

It may happen that interest groups or stakeholders need to be **COMMENT**
consulted when sorting out who is to go on the interviewing panel for
certain posts, particularly key ones in any organisation such as
directors, or specialist workers. It helps to have a clear policy worked
out in advance to diffuse personal disappointment. The panel can
then be seen to have been chosen on the basis of objective criteria.

TIPS ON SELECTING THE PANEL

- Having a selection panel as opposed to an individual is in accordance with guidance by CRE, EOC and Institute of Personnel and Development.
- It is a good idea to expect all members of the panel to participate in preparing for the selection interview, including the shortlisting of candidates and the preparation of questions for interview.
- Decide your policy on criteria for membership of the selection panel in advance of the recruitment.
- Decide which level of seniority needs to be represented on each panel; director level, manager level, officer level.
- Decide what to do if panel members know any of the applicants personally or by reputation. In this case they should 'declare an interest' and ideally not be involved in the decision to interview or appoint. If this is not possible, then there must be very clear rules of conduct adhered to in the decision-making process.
- For example, try to bring an outsider onto the panel who doesn't know anyone or have any 'axe to grind', to balance the panel and ensure favouritism doesn't result. There must be absolutely no discussion of any person's qualities based on information that has not emerged during the selection process, or anecdotal evidence of performance in previous posts.

Sian arranges training on equal opportunities interviewing for staff **COMMENT**
and committee to ensure that more people are qualified for next
time.

19 SHORTLISTING II

How to do it

Adam at Alcohol Counselling Service (ACS) has decided on the panel for the selection of the new information officer: himself; Glenda, a member of the Management Committee who has specialist information skills; Paul, the chair of the Management Committee and Jasvinder who has computer database knowledge and works for another advice centre in the area.

When he is trying to get everyone together for shortlisting it becomes clear that this is not going to be possible because of holidays and other commitments. Paul cannot make any of the dates that the others can. Then Jasvinder mentions that he knows someone who is putting in for the job and has prior knowledge of his team working abilities which are poor, while his computing abilities are high. What should he do — rule himself out as a panel member? Adam holds his head in his hands and wishes fervently that he had never started the process!

OPTIONS Should Adam:

- insist that the whole panel gets together for the shortlisting?
- accept that they can't and meet with Paul beforehand to discuss the process and go through the shortlisting forms with him?
- ignore or act on the interest that has been declared?

ISSUES

- *Shortlisting should ideally be done in a meeting, so that people can discuss any disagreements about particular candidates. However, if it is difficult for everyone to meet, it is possible for people to draw up shortlists individually and then discuss disagreements over the phone, or individuals' lists can be left with the chair to represent each person's views.*
- *The essential criteria from the person specification form the basis of shortlisting. New criteria or changes to criteria should not be made at this stage.*

Adam recognises that the shortlisting procedure he wants to use **PLANNING** may be unfamiliar to people and desperately wants them all to meet together. However, the panel really can't. Three out of the four can meet, so he accepts this. He prepares papers explaining the system and the shortlisting forms, so that everyone can be prepared for the meeting.

He prepares a standard form with the criteria from the person specification written across the top of a sheet of paper and the applicants' numbers down one side. Each shortlister has a separate form and indicates a view as to whether they think the applicant meets each criterion: fully, partly or not at all. All shortlisters must follow the same procedures. Using the judgements, 'Fully Met', 'Partly Met' and 'Not Met' is simpler than a points system which is open to subjective scoring difficulties. The chair of the panel asks which candidates are definitely in, definitely out or borderline. A process of elimination then leads to the final shortlist.

The shortlist will then be selected on the basis of how well they meet the criteria.

Adam meets Paul separately and goes through the shortlisting **OUTCOME** principles and process with him, so that Paul can fill in his forms and send them back in time to be discussed at the shortlisting meeting.

Adam also meets Jasvinder and says that he can't accept any discussion of second-hand anecdotal evidence about a candidate. The shortlisting and interviewing will have to proceed on that basis. He points out that the person specification includes team working criteria and they will be testing this at interview if the person gets that far.

Adam now tells all the shortlisted candidates: **NEXT STEP**
- the format of the interview.
- whether it is a two-tier interview process, the interview dates and time of interview.
- how many interviewers there are and who they are.
- what they need to bring to the interview if anything.
- an idea of the range of question areas.
- how long the interview will last.
- information about travel and childcare expenses.
- access details.
- any selection tests.

TIPS ON SHORTLISTING

- If the recruitment has worked so far according to equal opportunities, the shortlist should produce a range of people who have had equal chances of inclusion. If most of the applicants were women, but most of the shortlist are men, for example, then Adam should suspect that something is wrong with his process, and take action to investigate further.

- Do not reject on the basis of assumptions about the relative abilities of men and women, or ability related to race, age or any criterion that does not appear on the person specification. This is where anonymous forms are particularly useful, as they remove any temptation to make judgements on the basis of names.

- Reasons for rejection and success should be documented on special recruitment monitoring forms designed for the purpose. Record the assessment and decisions of shortlisting panels in relation to the relevant criteria.

- All application forms and related materials should be retained for six months after the shortlisting date in order to be able to be in a position to deal with any subsequent complaints about the implementation of your selection decisions.

LEGAL ASPECTS OF SHORT-LISTING

Even if you have taken positive action measures under the Race Relations Act or Sex Discrimination Act, you are still not allowed to discriminate at the point of selection. Once the applications arrive on your desk you must treat them all in the same way, applying selection criteria objectively.

Never discriminate at the point of selection unless you have used a Genuine Occupational Qualification for a male or female or a member of a particular ethnic group. Only then can you shortlist people of that race or sex only.

continued

Caselaw Webster v Kirklees Metropolitan Council

A white man who was not shortlisted for a council racial equal opportunities post was discriminated against on racial grounds. The tribunal found that some of the white male applicants (none of whom was shortlisted) were just as well qualified as those who were shortlisted.

The tribunal also found that the selection procedure had been open to abuse; one of the panel members had failed to 'declare an interest' and had shortlisted people known to them.

20 SELECTION TESTS — SKILLS BASED

Measuring skills and abilities

Adam of Alcohol Counselling Service (ACS) is trying to work out how best to measure three criteria in the person specification for the post of Information Officer. They are:

- Knowledge of the range of classification systems for information in the voluntary sector.
- Writing and communication skills.
- Ability to work constructively in a team setting and to network co-operatively with other projects.

Adam and the selection panel had blithely put these in without really thinking through how they would be tested on the interview day. Now Adam is faced with devising some ways of measuring these one week before the interview. He wants to go beyond asking searching questions in the panel, and devise some other ways of measuring the candidates' skills.

OPTIONS Should Adam:

- design a written test for knowledge of the classification system?
- ask the candidates to do a presentation on what would be best to do?
- do an observed group test for team skills?

ISSUES

- *The British Psychological Society quotes the predictive validity co-efficients of 0.25 for structured interviews and 0.00 for unplanned interviews. This means that even the best interviews are only 25% more accurate than picking names out of a hat.*
- *Job simulation exercises achieve the best validity rating in selection techniques and a combination of different techniques achieves the highest rating of all.*
- *Using a variety of methods gives the best result since it allows individuals to shine in different areas where they may have different personal preferences.*

Adam decides that he wants to have a written test, a presentation **ACTION** and a set of prepared scenarios that the candidates then have to talk through.

He devises:

1. A written test that the candidates are sent beforehand to test their knowledge of the range of classification systems. This lists the headings of the existing classification system that ACS uses and asks the candidates where they would add three new topics that have come along.

   This aims to test: that candidates are aware of different ways of classifying information; their approach to needs of enquirers; how they justified what they did — was it logical and did it take users' needs into account?

2. To test writing and communication skills as well as knowledge of an issue in information work, Adam sends out the following task which the candidates have to do before the interview and bring the finished work with them.

   "The Management Committee has asked for a position paper on setting up a loans management system for reference material. What points and arguments would you put forward for ACS setting one up? (2 sides of A4 maximum)."

   This should test candidates' attitudes to access to material, charging policy, clarity of writing and ability to be brief. It could be used as the basis of a short presentation.

3. To test team working abilities, Adam develops a set of three scenarios for team dilemmas that are given out on the day half an hour before the interview. The candidates are given half an hour to frame their responses in brief and talk about them in the interview.

   "What would you do if:

   A) A staff member asked you to help with an urgent mailing, but this conflicted with your getting one of your urgent priorities finished that the team director had asked you for by 4.00pm that day. If you say yes you can only complete it by missing a lunch date with your ex-partner in town that has been arranged for a month (and cannot be rearranged at short notice).

   B) A member of the team is persistent in complaining about another member of the team behind that person's back and wants to draw you into this.

C) A team member (in an all white team) makes stereotypical comments about the number of Asian men who are joining the counselling service. "I thought Muslims weren't supposed to drink anyway!" in a sneering tone. What would you do in response to this?"

The answers will give evidence of team negotiation skills, awareness of confidentiality issues, team rights and responsibilities, equal opportunities in practice and prioritising.

COMMENT   *Using the tests and the further questions in the interview, Adam has devised a variety of measures to test the person specification criteria. The more varied the measures that are used in selection the better; this increases the validity of the process.*

TIPS ON SELECTION TESTS

- It is good to use a variety of measures in your selection of candidates; this increases objectivity.

- Tests must be designed to show something of relevance to the criteria you are trying to measure. You need to be sure what answers you are looking for and how the test results will be scored or weighted in the decision-making process. Will one person only record the scoring and weighting or the whole panel?

- You may ask candidates to give a short presentation to the panel based on information you have previously supplied. Presentations are particularly useful in evaluating candidates' ability to group complex information and draw out the crucial points, ability to communicate and ability to argue a case.

- If it is reasonable for you to expect applicants to have certain specialist knowledge, then ask them to solve problems that test that piece of knowledge.

- Appropriate tests for manager candidates include decision-making scenarios and exercises in delegating and prioritising.

- Word processing and editing skills can also be tested in a practical exercise.

NEXT STEP   Adam tells the selectors how each person specification criterion will be tested and includes copies of the tests he has devised.

21 SELECTION TESTS — PSYCHOLOGICAL

Psychometric testing

One of the Management Committee members of RESCROFT has copied an article he came across in one of his personnel management magazines about psychometric testing. The article discusses how to do it and what the potential benefits are. He then phones Carmel and says that testing is carried out routinely by large companies, and if they put good money, even a lot of money, into it then it may be worthwhile. Does she think it is worth investigating for recruitment in the future — especially care workers where personality of the worker is so important?

Carmel's initial reaction is instinctively to say no. What she has heard about these tests is that they are glorified intelligence tests and can be developed only for large companies because they are designed specifically for certain aptitudes. She also has reservations about the equal opportunities impact of using such a test. How does this fit in with the person specification? Carmel is very concerned to get away from relying on perception of personality and towards as objective a measure of skills as possible.

Should Carmel: **OPTIONS**

- ignore the comments of the Management Committee member - they are only meddling?
- investigate cursorily, but not spend too much time on it?
- get her deputy to look into the issues and do a side of A4 for the Management Committee to consider.

- *Carmel should take the concerns of her Management Committee* **ISSUES**
  seriously, and if she can't answer the question herself, then maybe it is time she informed herself more about testing.
- *Psychometric testing is routinely carried out by large companies for screening graduate recruits for suitability for management.*
- *They are often used as part of a package of tests including aptitude tests and observed group tests.*

- *Psychometric tests are a measure of a psychological construct which produces scores which are reliable and which can be validated. They measure particular human characteristics and are usually one of two kinds. Tests of ability cover aptitude; cognitive tests cover the use of logic to solve a problem, verbal ability or numeracy. These tests must all be carried out in the same way under test conditions that are the same for all candidates. Finally, they are scored according to the publishers' system.*

ACTION   Carmel delegates one of her project managers to find out about these tests. The manager phones up the CRE and EOC and gets booklets from one of the major companies that designs them. They find out how much they would have to pay for the test and that they would have to get a person trained to give the tests under controlled conditions and to learn how to score them. This could potentially be a very expensive exercise.

OUTCOME   Carmel presents her findings to the Management Committee. They decide that the evidence for any extra benefit for good recruitment of a psychometric test is limited. They are concerned about the implications for equal opportunities. Paying a lot of money for a test and having a person trained in carrying out the test from a particular company is too great an expense for a limited reward.

TIPS ON PSYCHOMETRIC TESTS

- Tests are generally not relevant for the voluntary sector because:
  - They need to be normed using large populations of people from a variety of ethnic groups.
  - They are not relevant for one-off recruitments.
  - They rely on personality or intelligence being a valid measure of aptitude.
  - They need a trained person to administer them, so either you pay for one of your staff to be trained or you have to buy in the skill.
- It is widely believed that these tests measure intrinsic talents irrespective of ethnic, social and cultural background and experience. However, there is little evidence to support this and much to show that they contain unjustifiable cultural bias. Differences in social, educational and cultural experiences of people from different ethnic groups can often result in disparities in test performances.

Carmel reinforces the approach to selection she is taking, which is **NEXT STEP** to stress the importance of closely defining the person specification and deciding ways to measure those skills and abilities effectively.

There has been much debate about the degree to which tests are **LEGAL** proof against accusations of unfair discrimination against minority **ASPECTS** groups and women. **OF USING TESTS**

The Code of practice on Racial Discrimination says:
> "Selection tests which contain irrelevant questions or exercises on matters which may be unfamiliar to racial minority applicants should not be used (for example general knowledge questions on matters more likely to be familiar to the indigenous population)."

Using a test developed by a professional industrial psychologist trained in psychometrics and correctly administered is not sufficient to prove that no unfair discrimination has taken place. In addition to the validation process, you need to norm the test on ethnic minority workers. This will be difficult when the ethnic minority population is small in the workforce.

The recent CRE report into London Underground's use of selection tests concludes:
> "Our report draws attention to the use of psychological tests for job selection in a multi-racial labour market, and demonstrates that employers cannot assume that a generally reliable test will be equally reliable for a particular population or for a particular job. They must first check if the tests were designed for and tried out on a similarly diverse population and if the results had a racially discriminatory pattern. Second, employers must make sure that the tests measure precisely the skills and abilities needed for the job. Any mismatch here will mean inefficient and possibly discriminatory selection."

22 AVOIDING STEREOTYPING

Putting safeguards in place

Sian at the National Organisation of Health Promotion (NOHP) is aware that the selection process provides many danger points where stereotypes, prejudices, direct or indirect discrimination can be brought into play by the selectors. Sometimes this may be deliberate and conscious, at other times it may be due to unconscious perceptions. She is slightly concerned about a member of the selection panel elected from the Management Committee. She is Jean, a retired doctor, old-fashioned in some attitudes, and particularly about women's childcare responsibilities. She thinks that people with children should be at home looking after them. Sian has had to tackle her on more than one occasion about this, but suspects that she still harbours this view. She wonders if she can be relied on in the interview not to ask questions only of women about childcare, which she knows is against the law.

OPTIONS Should Sian:

- arrange training for all the selectors on equal opportunities interviewing?
- get them all together before the interview and explain about indirect discrimination and stereotyping herself?
- pull Jean aside and have a frank discussion with her about the legal requirements of not asking discriminatory questions?

ISSUES
- *The first hurdle is to accept that we all have stereotypes and prejudices about something. We make judgements about people all the time on the basis of how they look, what clothes they wear, how they speak. If these attitudes are not to affect our attempts to select according to equal opportunities principles, then they have to be brought out into the open and a system has to be designed to counteract them.*
- *The main dangers in selection are from prejudice, stereotyping, unequal treatment, and particular perceptions. See **Definitions** at end of this section.*

- *Always interview with a group of people from varied races, different genders and backgrounds; so that there is less chance of uni-cultural stereotypes operating.*

Sian decides that she will organise training before the interviews **PLANNING** because it is important that all selectors are aware of the potential for bias and stereotyping. She knows about one person's potential prejudices but little about the views of other selectors.

She discusses carefully with three potential trainers how they **ACTION** would handle this issue in a training course and picks the one that seems most relevant to the circumstances of her organisation. The trainer will be using role plays and video material to highlight how stereotyping operates and will address the legal position on questioning techniques to avoid discrimination.

Sian seems to have pre-empted a potentially difficult interviewing **COMMENT** *situation. She has identified the issue as a training need for the whole panel to work on, since everyone has prejudices, some are just more aware of them and up-front about them than others.*

TIPS ON AVOIDING STEREOTYPING

- To avoid stereotyping and bias, follow as systematic a process as possible.
- Get training that highlights your own prejudices and potentially discriminatory practices.
- Develop clear criteria for assessment based on the person specification which has been derived from clear job analysis.
- Select in a systematic fashion.
- Design questions and tests to elicit the information you require about how well candidates meet the person specification.
- Ask candidates the same questions in a similar way — avoid directly or indirectly discriminatory questions.
- Record the answers systematically.
- Decide on the basis of information given and displayed ability to do the job, not on the basis of gut feelings that cannot to be explained in terms of skills or abilities.

NEXT STEP Sian highlights areas of the recruitment process towards which she wants to change her organisation's policy in the light of what she has learnt. She makes sure that more of the staff and Management Committee are booked on suitable training later in the year, in order to raise the skills base in the organisation.

DEFINITIONS Perceptions

We weigh people up, we use our 'gut feelings' or 'sixth sense' about new people. These feelings are called our *perceptions* of others. They are conditioned by our history, upbringing, sex, race, class, culture and are highly subjective.

Distortions

Distortions of perception are particularly likely when interviewing people of different social background, culture or gender from one's own. Their roots are deeply embedded in the selector. However, being aware of the nature of such psychological processes is important in order to change your behaviour to counteract them. We all have them and we can learn to overcome them, once we have recognised they are in operation.

The perception effects listed below may involve stereotyping and prejudice. These are effects, observed under test conditions, which have been shown to affect the performance of selectors.

Assumed Similarity Effect: This occurs where an interviewer establishes common ground with the candidate in certain ways which may be irrelevant to the job, and generalises this to other areas, which may be selection criteria. This reinforces a tendency to recruit in one's own image.

For example, preferring a candidate whose CV records them as having worked in a certain organisation, because you have too. "This candidate worked for the Children's Society and so have I, therefore this candidate will be a good youth worker, just as I am."

Primacy Effect: The 'Primacy Effect' allows the first impression to influence the judgement of the candidate overall. For example, if the candidate gives a poor answer to a question in the first topic area or has a real weakness in one area, it does not mean that the candidate may not have good experience in other areas.

Halo Effect: The 'Halo Effect' allows the favourable impression made by one trait to influence the judgement of other traits.

Prejudice

This underlies preferences, attitudes, judgements and opinions formed without adequate knowledge or reason. If you make your decision on the basis of personal preference or opinion, you may well exclude someone from a job they would be perfectly good at. You should try not to have a fixed idea about how a job should be done or who would be suitable for it. You should base your decision only on whether the person has the right capability.

Stereotyping

This means generalisation — often derogatory and based on prejudice — about any group. It can be used to prejudge a whole group on the basis of one individual and it can transfer one person's preconceived views of a group onto individual members of that group.

Stereotyping means that you assume things about people because they belong to a particular group. For example, some people still believe that women with children are 'unreliable', and they are less likely to employ them for that reason.

Unequal treatment

This means unfair or unequal treatment of individuals because of their classification under the headings gender, race, ethnic group, age, etc.

23 PREPARING FOR PANEL INTERVIEWS

For Carmel in RESCROFT the interviews for the deputy manager post are one week away. Since she has decided to use both an internal appointment system and positive action measure (Genuine Occupational Qualification), and both of these have not been used before by RESCROFT, she decides to work out if she needs to do anything different for the panel interviews. There have been three internal applicants and all are suitably qualified, so the panel will be interviewing all of them.

OPTIONS Should Carmel:

- go through exactly the same process she would if this were an external recruitment?

- consider doing some internal information giving about the new policies and processes to allay any possible mis-information about what the new systems are, why they have been introduced and how they will apply in the future?

- use fewer people on the interview panel because it is an internal appointment?

ISSUES
- *Carmel has landed herself in a delicate position, bringing in two new policies at the same time.*

- *There may well be a need for an internal information session so that other staff know there is no question of favouritism or nepotism occurring, and to go through the reasons for using the Genuine Occupational Qualification.*

- *It is a good idea to bring onto the panel a completely impartial outsider with the relevant skills and knowledge in order to avoid any question of the selection being stitched up.*

- *The normal process for interviews at this level in the organisation should be followed.*

Carmel drafts and circulates the internal appointments policy **PLANNING**
document. Then she briefs her team leaders about the interview
format and the Genuine Occupational Qualification and asks them
to feed this down to their teams. She requests that team leaders
with workers who are applying for the post prepare to counsel staff
on reasons why they did not get the job, since two people (or
possibly three) will be disappointed.

Carmel prepares the package of information for the interviewers **ACTION**
who will be herself, Joseph, the manager of the project, and Kwesi,
a person already managing a similar local project for Asian elders.
She sends out:
- application forms.
- timetable of the interviews.
- interview grid.
- questions.
- job description.
- person specification.

She also organises the administration staff to:
- make sure someone is there to let people in, get them a cup of
   coffee, and deal with expenses and travel arrangements for
   external candidates.
- ensure they have an accurate list of names and times .
- put up warning notices to other staff/users that the interview
   room is in use.
- ensure the interviewers are not interrupted by phone calls etc.
- provide a glass of water in the interview room.
- provide adequate seating to give room to the applicant and an
   air of friendly formality.

Carmel then sends out notices to the selection panel to meet in
advance and decide the following:
- the roles of each member.
- a clear plan of the shape of the interview.
- question areas.
- specific sample questions .
- who should ask which ones .
- the beginning and ending process.
- how notetaking will be done.

At the end of the meeting the panel has addressed all the above **OUTCOME**
issues and have a clear role for the chair who:
- makes introductions.
- explains the process of the interview.

continued

- tells the candidate if questions can be asked on the way
through or at the end.
- moves the questioning on .
- keeps the flow going and keeps the interview to time.
- deals with problems or irrelevances.
- chairs the responses to the applicants' questions.
- closes the interview and says what will happen next.
- chairs the deciding discussion.
- reminds the panel of appropriate body language, and paying
attention to the interviewee.

TIPS ON PANEL PREPARATION

- Panel preparation is well worth the time spent on it.
The panel will interview much more systematically
together, and will have had a chance to check out a
common position on equal opportunities questioning
techniques and decision-making techniques.

- If no internal applicant meets the person specification
after the interview, then the recruitment process must
be opened up externally as quickly as possible.

- If you use a Genuine Occupational Qualification,
once the application forms have landed on your desk,
you must shortlist only those from the relevant ethnic
background who meet the person specification.

- Once shortlisted, all candidates must be judged on
how well they meet the person specification criteria,
just as in a normal recruitment process.

- The preparation for interviews should not differ as
between internal candidates and external ones;
candidates still need to fill in an application form and
be shortlisted against the criteria.

- Any internal candidates not appointed should be
given a full explanation of why they did not get the
job and offered counselling on how they could bring
their skills up to the required standard to get a job of
a similar nature next time.

NEXT STEP   Carmel draws up an interview process sheet with question areas
and sample opening questions and who will ask each one.

24 QUESTIONING TECHNIQUE

What you can and can't ask in an interview

Carmel is in a selection panel meeting with the other two people who are selecting for the deputy project managerat RESCROFT: Joseph, the project manager, and Kwesi who works for another advice centre in the area.

The panel are meeting to decide both on the roles they will take in the interview and the questions they will ask.

As they proceed with the questions, they realise that there is a fundamental difference between Joseph and Kwesi. Joseph had some training on equal opportunities a few years ago through the local authority where he works and he was taught that every candidate had to be asked the same questions exactly and that there should be no follow-up questions or different ones, since this would be giving some candidates an unfair advantage.

Kwesi's argument is that it is not the questions themselves that have to be asked in exactly the same way word for word, but the question areas the panel will be asking about. They may define a starting question for each area, but if the candidate gets the wrong end of the stick or forgets the second half of the question and needs to have it paraphrased, then the panel should be able to do this.

The two of them get heated and Carmel decides to call for a tea break to calm everybody down, after which she will facilitate a discussion on the issue, not a shouting match.

Should Carmel: OPTIONS

- discuss the points Kwesi is making with him in the break and then pass these on to Joseph on his own?
- go back to the first principles of equal opportunities in recruitment and selection to consider if the proposed method is fair?

ISSUES • At the end of the interview, the panel need to know how well the candidate can meet the person specification criteria. This means that candidates must be questioned in a similar way under each area. However, it is more important to gain the relevant information than to stick to set questions and to ask only those questions. Some candidates may need supplementary or probing questions to give the information required, and their answers might lead along different paths in each case.

• Before the interview, the panel should draw up a framework of questions which applies to all candidates. These might cover:
— their current job or activity
— what particularly interests them about the job they are applying for
— skills and experience, expanding from the application form
— how a candidate might apply these in the job
— how particular situations might be tackled or how a candidate did tackle a particular event

• The question areas should be divided up according to expertise among the panel members and certain common questions agreed beforehand.

ACTION Carmel mediates between Joseph and Kwesi and together they decide on the questioning strategy that they will adopt. They follow the structure outlined above and end up with a question area for each section of the person specification and two tests. Then they each write two questions as starters for the area under consideration. For example:

"How would you deal with a project worker who repeatedly ignored an instruction?"

"Can you tell me which areas of supervision you expect to find most challenging?"

OUTCOME The interviews are successfully completed and Joseph comments how smoothly he felt they went. He had no qualms about the times when they varied the questioning routine.

COMMENT *Kwesi was right to stick to his guns on this issue. It is far more important for the interviewers to feel that they have got the information they need to assess the candidate against the person specification, than to stick to a rigid framework of questions.*

TIPS ON QUESTIONING TECHNIQUE

- All questions must be clearly related to requirements of the job (as described in the person specification).

- The substance of questions must not vary according to the perceived ethnic or national origins, disability, marital status, sexuality, age or any other characteristics attributed to the candidate.

- Candidates must not be asked questions about their personal circumstances or family commitments. For example, they must not be asked about their ethnic origin or that of their family, or how they would react to a colleague of a different race, sex or sexual orientation.

- Where a job involves unsocial or irregular hours or travel, the full facts must be presented in the job information to all applicants before the interview. The selection panel must establish by a simple question whether or not each candidate has understood the requirements of the job. Questions about domestic obligations must not be asked; they could be construed as showing bias against women.

- Don't let a vague or general, uninformative answer pass without a probe. Probing questions make the candidate give more detailed evidence.

  "When you produced final accounts, what form did they take?"
  "Exactly what percentage of your time is currently spent in training?"

- The panel should agree a procedure for other interviewers wishing to follow on from the main questioner on a particular topic.

Carmel writes up the structure of the interview into a plan of action **NEXT STEP** laid out with the question areas, the starting questions and who will ask them, with space for the interviewers to record their notes of the candidates' answers.

LEGAL ASPECTS OF INTER-VIEWS

Relate questions to the requirements of the job. Where it is necessary to assess how personal circumstances will affect performance of the job, discuss them objectively without reference to detailed questions based on assumptions about marital status, children and domestic obligations.

Case law: Woodhead case. The real issue in deciding whether questions are discriminatory or not must be based on what the employer needs to know. The issue is that the candidate is aware of the constraints of the job and can make effective plans to work within them. Employers do not need to know what those plans are nor should they make assumptions about the viability of those plans.

25 THE PANEL INTERVIEW PROCESS

How to interview together well

Sian's worst nightmare has come true in the panel interviews for the development officer job at the National Organisation of Health Promotion (NOHP). The panel [see *Scenario 18*] consists of Jean, a Management Committee member with very strong ideas about how the development work should be done who disapproves of women with young children working, Sohalia the existing development worker, and Sian herself.

Sian has arranged training for the panel, and has got them all together for preparation and discussion of questions and role. She has organised a final meeting on the day of the interviews to go through the pre-prepared questions and to check they all know what to do. But despite all this, in the first interview Jean has still asked one of the candidates: "Do you have children? Who will be looking after them while you are travelling round the country doing the development work?"

Should Sian:
OPTIONS

- stop the interview straight away and apologise?
- make an interjection and say that Jean has put the point badly and the reformulate what they intended to say?
- say nothing now, but halt the process before the next interview and discuss the issue with Jean and the others again, making clear the possibility of being taken to an industrial tribunal?

- *The panel needs to sort out beforehand a few clear rules and*   ISSUES
  principles so that everyone knows what is expected of them and how to avoid breaching equal opportunities legislation by introducing direct or indirect discrimination.
- *It is important to agree on the way the interview will flow and how panel members will act if they want to interrupt each other.*
- *The chair should be the most experienced interviewer, not necessarily the most senior person present.*
- *Interviews must be fair to all candidates.*

ACTION   Sian decides she has to intervene in the interview at that moment as she is aware of the potential consequences of the candidate making a complaint. She does it in as tactful a way as possible.

"Excuse me Jean, I would just like to put that point in a different way to Sarah [the candidate].

"Sarah, as we explained in the job information we sent out, sometimes you will need to travel away from London, stay overnight and spend approximately three days out of every five away from the office, travelling long distances in some cases. Will you be able to work in this way?"

The candidate seems a bit surprised by the interplay between the interviewers, but addresses her answer to Sian and ignores the glances from Jean to Sian. In the gap between that interview and the next Sian raises the issue with Jean again. Does she not understand that they could be taken to a tribunal for asking questions in this way?

OUTCOME   Fortunately the candidate does not press any charges about discriminatory interviewing. Sian is still furious that despite all her well laid plans this went wrong. However, her preparation was the best possible and her eventual intervention the most appropriate action.

TIPS ON PANEL PREPARATION

- Research shows the disadvantages of interviews to include:
  - Prior knowledge about the applicant will bias the interviewers' evaluation.
  - Interviewers have a stereotype of what constitutes a 'good' applicant.
  - Interviewers tend to favour applicants who share their own attitudes.
  - The order in which applicants are interviewed will influence evaluations.
  - The order in which information is elicited will influence evaluations.
  - Negative information is weighted unduly highly.
  - Interviewers come to a decision very early on in the interview.
  - Interviewers forget much of the content of the interview minutes after it has finished.

continued

TIPS ON PANEL PREPARATION (continued)

- Despite their drawbacks, interviews are still widely used and it is important to maximise their benefit.

- If an interviewer says something potentially discriminatory, it is very important to leap in and say something to correct the mistake. If you don't, you could run the risk of being taken to a tribunal.

- Guidelines for effective interviews:
  - Make suitable arrangements for any candidates with disabilities prior to the interview.
  - Make notes during the interview so that you don't forget key points. Obviously, don't have your head down the whole time!
  - Avoid very short interviews: extending them from 15 to 30 minutes prevents the interviewer from coming to a premature decision.
  - Avoid spending too long on the earlier part of the interview and then running out of time to probe as thoroughly as is needed on the key issues of how well the candidate will perform the tasks.
  - Base assessments upon factual evidence of past performance, behaviour and achievements.
  - Arrange for candidates to be assessed by a panel rather than by one person alone.

- Ensure that the panel take regular breaks so that they do not become too tired themselves during the interview day.

- Record the reasons why candidates were not appointed.

Sian has a full and frank discussion with Jean about her suitability as a Management Committee member, since she has gone against Sian's wishes and the expressed policy of NOHP on equal opportunities interviewing, in spite of training. She receives Jean's resignation letter a week later. **NEXT STEP**

It is against the law to ask questions in the interview which are likely to result in indirect or direct discrimination. **LEGAL ASPECTS OF INTERVIEWS**

26 MAKING THE DECISION

Who gets the job?

Carmel at RESCROFT has been interviewing all day for the deputy manager job. There were three internal candidates who all met the Genuine Occupational Qualification of being African-Caribbean, and met the other criteria in the person specification. She has been interviewing with Joseph the project manager and Kwesi, a manager from an associated project outside of RESCROFT.

The panel have now come to the decision-making part of the process. They have consulted their notes and have all completed the interview-marking form that Carmel has circulated. This form is similar to the one used in the shortlisting process, with names across the top and the person specification criteria down one side with their associated question areas or tests.

Carmel asks them to spend time filling in the forms marking each criterion *Fully Met*, *Partly Met* or *Not Met*. There are 10 criteria on the sheet. Once they have all consulted their notes and filled in the forms on their own, Carmel gathers them up and amalgamates the scores onto one sheet. No one has scored a Not Met. Jennifer has scored 5 Partly Mets and Ben and Lisa have scored 8 Fully Mets each. Ben and Lisa have effectively tied for top place. Carmel tells the panel. Now what should they do?

OPTIONS Should Carmel:

- go back over the marking and see if there are any differences in the scores given to Ben and Lisa that might merit discussion?
- toss a coin to see who gets the job?
- re-interview Ben and Lisa as soon as possible, refining the questions under the two criteria that they scored as Partly Met?
- begin to make judgements about how they would do the job, since they are known to members of the panel, rather than keeping the discussion to how they performed in the interview?

- *Where candidates' ratings are very close in a selection process, advocates of those candidates could request to re-examine the ratings on specific criteria, each putting forward arguments. If other members are convinced by such arguments, which must be substantiated by evidence, then they can revise their rating. If panel members are not convinced, no change should be made. All arguments must be fully backed up by assessment of evidence, not just impressions. Revision of any score can only be on the grounds of error in interpreting data against criteria.*
- *The above should be done only if the rating is close, otherwise there is no need for discussion, unless there is a glaring error in interpreting data against essential criteria.*
- *The decision should be made by consensus if possible; if not, the panel should vote.*

ISSUES

The panel decide to review the *Partly Met* scores for Ben and Lisa to see if there are any discrepancies in the method of scoring. It turns out that Kwesi has misinterpreted something Lisa said and scored her *Partly Met* instead of *Fully Met* on one answer. The panel then checks carefully back over all its scoring, especially of *Partly Met*, and comes up with the new result of Lisa with one *Partly Met* and Ben with two. This means that although they are very close, Lisa has technically more weight in her favour than Ben.

ACTION

The panel decide to offer the job to Lisa and delegate Carmel to talk to both Lisa and Ben about the outcome of the interviews. She will go through the process in some detail with Ben to ensure he sees it as a positive learning experience as far as possible.

OUTCOME

If both of them had still scored the same, the panel decided that they would have re-interviewed them both with additional, more rigorous tests for the areas of the person specification where they were most unsure about the candidates' abilities

---

TIPS ON MAKING THE DECISION

- Make a decision immediately the interviews have been completed.
- The panel should make a first and a second choice where possible in case the preferred candidate turns the job down or has unsatisfactory references.
- If sufficient doubt arises between two candidates, see them again.

continued

TIPS ON MAKING THE DECISION (continued)

- It is very important for equal opportunities not to let bias creep in at the very final stage. For example, it is not acceptable to rank an able-bodied person above a person with a disability, or a single parent with childcare needs below a non-parent, owing to the extra cost of meeting their needs, when they are of equal rank in all other respects.

- Where there is doubt about the suitability of a candidate because of the nature of a disability, further advice must be taken about the disability and the availability of aids to employment or the adaptation of buildings before a decision to reject is taken.

- Selection decisions must not be influenced either by the traditional sexual or racial profile of the postholder or by any colleague's expressed unwillingness to work with, for example, a lesbian.

- If any members of the interview panel feel that discrimination has occurred in the selection process, the matter must be reported direct to the Management Committee. No selection decision should be made until the issue is resolved. Candidates must be told of any delay.

- Staff involved in showing people round and who are not on the interview panel should not have any say in who is appointed.

- The panel need to be clear about why people were not selected, and notes should be made of this during the decision-making process.

- The panel may decide to appoint no-one. Perhaps the adverts, job descriptions, application forms or person specifications were not well thought out, or the level of pay is too low for the responsibility of the job. If this happens the job will have to be re-advertised.

- All application forms and interview notes must be kept for at least six months after the end of the recruitment action, so that any consequent enquiries or disputes can be adequately handled. Monitoring forms must be kept indefinitely.

Carmel arranges to see the successful candidate with an offer letter **NEXT STEP**
and arranges for the managers of the two unsuccessful candidates
to talk to them.

Making decisions unfairly is the area that attracts most cases to **LEGAL**
industrial tribunal. You must be very careful to record the reasons **ASPECTS**
why people were given jobs or not and keep interview notes and **OF**
material for at least six months afterwards. **MAKING**
THE
DECISION

27 REFERENCES

Checking on your chosen candidate

Sian has to take up two references each for the top two people on the interview list for the post at National Organisation of Health Promotion (NOHP) . She knows there has been some debate recently about the value of taking up references. How can she make sure she gets a clear picture of their work history without an anodyne response? Is it just going through the motions when candidates inevitably give you a referee they know will be favourable?

OPTIONS Should Sian:

- not bother to take up references — they are always exaggerated?
- take up references over the phone and confirm in writing?
- take them up in writing and confirm over the phone?

ISSUES • *Taking up references in a structured fashion and asking questions that are specifically job-related is worthwhile. General references and references taken over the phone, with no record of who said what to whom, are not suitable.*

- *It is much better, when writing for a reference, to structure the letter in relation to the person specification so that a specific question is asked for each specific criterion on the person specification.*

- *The sickness record of the candidate over the last year should be asked about. Also confirm that the candidate works there in the position and on the terms stated and ask about reasons for leaving.*

*[See **Appendix X: Sample reference request**.]*

PLANNING Sian writes out a list of questions she wants answered about the person and writes a letter to the referees. She says in the letter that she would like to contact them by phone over the next three days to take up a verbal reference, following her guidelines in the letter; but that she will still need confirmation in writing.

Sian makes the phone calls and gets through to all four referees. **ACTION**
Three of the responses are generally favourable, but one is
worrying. This is from the second last workplace of the first choice
candidate. The referee was not positive about the person's ability
to be clear about priorities or stick to them. She also hinted at
personality difficulties between the candidate and the team. When
questioned more closely she said that no disciplinary action had
been taken, but that the candidate had strong views that others
found difficult to deal with. Sian asks her to put this in writing.

Sian now has two very positive references for the second choice **OUTCOME**
candidate and one positive for the first choice plus this worrying
feedback. There is quite a degree of difference between the first and
second choice, so she would prefer to take the first choice if she can.
After consulting the chair she decides to:

1. Re-interview the good referee of the first choice candidate about
   the specific points mentioned. She gets the feedback that the
   candidate does have strong opinions, but that the referee had
   not found her disruptive to the team, and that her standard of
   work was good. Sian considers that she herself is a strong team
   manager with no qualms about setting boundaries and dealing
   with workers in the more detached development role.

2. Ask the candidate about the reference and get her version of
   events.

3. After this discussion Sian feels confident in the candidate's skills
   and in her own ability to manage her, so she decides to proceed
   to an offer, subject to a stringent probationary period.

Sian consults the chair of the Committee and proceeds to make an
offer and reject unsuitable candidates.

Sian has to be clear about her ability to manage someone with strong **COMMENT**
opinions and her management skills generally. There is no point in
taking on a person who is good in the job but too much of a maverick
for the organisation to be able to manage satisfactorily.

TIPS ON REFERENCES

Telephone references

- If you are in a great rush to make an offer of appointment, it can be acceptable to phone the referees with the candidate's permission.

- You must go through a structured list of questions based on what you would ask for in a written reference letter.

- Always follow-up the telephone reference with a request for a written reference as well.

- Make sure you are speaking to the relevant person and try to talk to the line manager who knows the candidate's work very well.

Written references

- References labelled 'without prejudice' or 'without legal responsibility' imply that the writer will take no responsibility for decisions you may make on the basis of them.

- Always investigate an unsatisfactory reference.

- Check qualifications if they form part of the essential person specification criteria.

- Keep all written information and interview notes, application forms etc for at least six months (three years in Northern Ireland).

LEGAL ASPECTS OF REFERENCES

Duty of Care

You are not obliged by law to give a reference for any employee. However, references, if given should be accurate, and must not be negligent or mislead by omission. You have an obligation to ensure that no individual or organisation suffers because you failed to take care when giving a reference.

Discrimination in references

Don't ask questions about a black or woman candidate that you wouldn't ask about other candidates. It is illegal to discriminate directly or indirectly in the arrangements you make for determining who should be offered employment.

continued

Do not make a blanket request for information regarding convictions. Where references mention spent or unrelated convictions they should be ignored. Employers who act on information about a spent conviction (except for those jobs exempted under the Rehabilitation of Offenders Act) will be committing an unlawful act.

References and confidentiality

If the reference becomes the subject of a defamation or discrimination case then the court or Industrial Tribunal can order it to be disclosed. If references are stored on computer then the subject has rights of access to refer to them by virtue of the Data Protection Act.

Police checks

It may also be necessary to carry out a police check on candidates for jobs that are not exempt under the Rehabilitation of Offenders Act, for example, some professions such as accountant, or people working with children.

28 THE OFFER LETTER

What to put in the letter offering the job

Sian of National Organisation of Health Promotion (NOHP) , having recently taken up references for the development worker job discovered a potential area of difficulty in the chosen candidate's strong personality. Sian thinks that she can manage her successfully, but wants to provide herself with a let-out if it all goes horribly wrong and the new worker disrupts the smooth working of the team. Having decided to make an offer of appointment to the candidate, she wants to attach a more stringent probationary period than is normally operated by NOHP.

OPTIONS **Should Sian:**

- go ahead and vary the terms of employment from the normal ones for a regular worker at NOHP?
- offer the same contract but make clear the differences in the offer letter?

ISSUES
- *There is no obligation on an organisation to offer exactly the same terms of employment to all its employees, although it could obviously affect motivation and morale if all workers were on completely different terms and conditions.*
- *The contents of a letter of appointment form part of the employment contract together with the statement of terms and conditions, any other relevant documents and custom and practice.*
- *You have to be careful exactly what you put in an offer letter as terms of employment and to refer to other documents where necessary, for example the contract, the staff handbook, the discipline and grievance procedure, health and safety rules.*
- *In the offer letter you should add any conditions to which the offer itself is subject and a clear timescale within which the employee is expected to get back to you with acceptance or rejection of the offer.*
- *If the prospective employee negotiates on any terms in the offer letter and you agree, then make sure that the final version is the one signed and accepted by both parties.*

Sian wants to offer the standard contract terms except in one **PLANNING**
particular: the probationary period. At present NOHP operates a
six month probationary period which is extendible to up to nine
months. Sian wants to reduce this to four months extendible to six
months because of her anxiety over the reference.

Sian consults the chair and proceeds to draft the offer letter and **ACTION**
amends the probationary period.

The candidate wants to take up this job. She feels a bit insulted **OUTCOME**
about the outcome of the references and that she should be
subjected to this additional stringency. However, she decides that
she will accept this point. She wants to negotiate a slight change to
the flexible working terms so that she can ensure being able to pick
up her children from school. The core hours are at present 9.30am –
4.00pm. These would not allow her to collect her children because
of the travel time, so she is asking for her core hours to be 9.00am –
3.30pm. When Sian hears about this, she smiles to herself, thinking
'This is her way of saying "You may put terms onto me, but I want
to put terms onto you".'

Sian phones up a day or so after sending the letter to discuss the
terms with the candidate. She negotiates on the one point about
flexitime and then finalises the appointment, having reissued an
amended offer letter to the candidate.

Sian is right to want to safeguard herself and the organisation from her **COMMENT**
own and the selection panel's possible poor judgement. Probationary
periods are a very important way of ensuring that mistakes made by
the appointment panel can be undone as painlessly as possible. It is
better to sever the ties sooner rather than later as long as you have
proceeded with a proper induction and probation period and are
convinced that the person either does not have the necessary skills or
in some other way cannot meet the requirements of the post.

TIPS ON OFFERS

- Always make your offer in careful terms; the letter of
  appointment is part of the contract for legal purposes.
- Write down points rather than relying on custom and
  practice.
- Ensure all changes to terms by negotiation are written
  down.

LEGAL ASPECTS OF OFFERS Follow the offer letter with written terms and conditions. All employees working for eight hours or more per week who have at least one month's service are entitled to receive written terms and conditions within two months of starting work (Trade Union Reform and Employment Rights Act 1993).

29 UNSUCCESSFUL CANDIDATES

Adam has just taken a difficult phone call from a person who came to the interviews for the information officer at Alcohol Counselling Service (ACS), but who was not offered the job. He is a white male, and the successful candidate is a black woman. He is suggesting that she was only taken on because she was black and that he has more qualifications than her to do the job. He says that he will be consulting his union rep and see if he can take ACS to an industrial tribunal. Adam blanches and reiterates the reasons why the candidate did not get the job as clearly as he can. He has already written these out in a letter, but the rejected candidate is too furious and abusive to listen.

The reasons were that although he had better computer skills than the appointed candidate he failed to score as well on other main points on the person specification. He did not perform as well in the tests on writing skills or on team work. (See *Scenario 20: Selection Tests — Skills Based.*)

Should Adam: OPTIONS

- do nothing — wait for the letter from the Industrial Tribunal?
- inform the chair and check that the panel have kept all the notes and information from the interviews that they should have?
- re-convene the panel to reconsider their decision?
- panic and offer to pay off the disappointed candidate?

- *If a person suspects that they have been discriminated against on*   ISSUES
  grounds of their race or sex and suffered a detriment in the
  selection process or selection decision then they have a right to
  make a claim to an Industrial Tribunal (IT). The claim must be
  made within three months of the decision having been made.

- *The law is clear that where a complainant has been interviewed*
  but not appointed, and suspects discrimination, then the
  complainant can request that the interviewing panel disclose all
  relevant documents including interview notes, application forms of
  all candidates, rejection letters etc.

PLANNING   Adam contacts the chair of the Management Committee and gathers all the information together from the interviews. They go through it together and as far as they can tell they should be able to prove that the decision was made on fair grounds. They wait to see if the person was bluffing or not. Adam has heard somewhere that more men than women and more white than black people actually claim discrimination!

ACTION   The rejected candidate has filled out an IT1 form within the time limit of three months and sent this to the Secretary of Tribunals. Adam receives a 'Notice of Appearance' form (IT3). He has to send this back within 14 days saying whether he is going to resist the claim of discrimination and on what grounds he bases his defence.

At this stage Adam sends the person specification and the final scoring sheet for decision-making by the selectors. He then gets a notice to disclose to the tribunal information on the interviews and notes made by selectors. Following that, he gets notice to attend a conciliation meeting with ACAS (the Advisory, Conciliation and Arbitration Service) and the aggrieved candidate.

OUTCOME   The outcome of the conciliation is that the candidate is persuaded that rejection was due to the way the other person met the criteria, rather than any discrimination on grounds of race or sex. He is still disgruntled, but the ACAS officer points out that he would be highly unlikely to succeed in any further proceedings. Adam heaves a huge sigh of relief and heads back to the office.

COMMENT   Adam escaped going to a full tribunal because ACS had scrupulously selected the best person for the job against all the person specification criteria. He had kept all the relevant documentation and information and so was able to back up his case easily.

NEXT STEP   Adam makes sure that the organisation's recruitment and selection policy includes all the necessary steps to take and points out to other members of the selection panel and the Management Committee the penalties of failing to follow the rules.

102

TIPS ON REJECTING CANDIDATES

- Be very clear in your selection process not to discriminate unfairly to achieve a 'balance' in the team of white/black or men/women. The possible consequences of a person bringing a successful claim of discrimination against you are a large fine and bad publicity.

- Telling people they have not been selected is an area that requires some care and attention. It is always difficult to tell someone that they haven't got a job and it is polite and lessens the blow to send a more personal rather than a standard letter.

- Don't keep more people hanging on longer than necessary. Tell them when and how you will let them know at the end of the interview and then follow that procedure.

- Be prepared to talk to people.

- Do always be clear about the reasons for rejection in a letter.

REJECTION OF AN EX-OFFENDER

If an ex-offender's application has been unsuccessful, then you need to be particularly careful about saying why. Standard letters of rejection may reinforce the assumptions by ex-offenders with spent convictions that there is no point in disclosing information. Details about the applicant's convictions should always be kept highly confidential.

- The applicant should be told if rejection was because a conviction was considered job-related.

- If the applicant did not handle the disclosure of a previous conviction very well, then it would be helpful for the interviewer to give feedback on this.

- Records should be kept of the results of interviews so that employers are able to review their selection and recruitment procedures.

LEGAL ASPECTS OF REJECTION

Discrimination in not offering employment

If a woman, man, married person or person from one of the ethnic minorities, or person of a particular religion or political belief in Northern Ireland thinks that they have been discriminated against in the selection process or in the selection decision, they can make a claim to an Industrial Tribunal. This claim must be made within three months of the decision.

If a tribunal finds that discrimination has occurred it may order the company to put matters right and may award damages for hurt feelings.

Case law: Noone v North West Thames Regional Health Authority.

*The complainant, from Sri Lanka, applied for a post as a consultant microbiologist: she was interviewed, but not appointed. She had better qualifications, experience and publications than the appointed candidate. Her complaint of direct race discrimination was upheld. The Court of Appeal ruled that the inference of discrimination was correct because her application was stronger than that of the appointed candidate and **the employer was unable to give a satisfactory reason for having rejected her after interview.***

30 INDUCTION

Ensuring a successful transition into a new job

The new deputy manager at RESCROFT, Daria, who was recruited as an internal candidate, has just had her first probation review meeting after three months in post. She complained to Joseph her manager that she has not had a proper induction and that it is unfair to assess her now. Joseph comes to Carmel, the Director, and says that he feels Daria is not entirely up to the standard he had hoped, but that could possibly be because of lack of induction. She has been a bit reluctant to take on a proper supervisory role. Carmel questions him more closely about what has happened. Joseph says that he didn't bother too much about induction because as an internal candidate she had already been working for RESCROFT for two years. He was on holiday for three weeks and then she was away for two weeks, so they have had only three supervision sessions during the first three months.

Should Carmel: **OPTIONS**

- harangue Joseph for not taking the induction period seriously?
- insist that the probationary period has to stand and that if the new worker is not up to standard, then she has to be demoted back to a project worker?
- extend the probation period and coach Joseph on how to do the induction better?

- *Starting a new job should not turn out to be a form of endurance*   **ISSUES**
  test or baptism of fire, separating the 'women from the girls' or the like. Nothing will sooner alienate an employee. So it is important to induct people properly — or face the consequences.
- *Induction can involve two aspects: the content of the work and the context of the work. Bear in mind that there is a lot to take in and people can get rapidly saturated with overload of information. Some people change employment infrequently and may have greater difficulty: for example, women returners or people coming into the workforce after time off.*

- *Set a steady pace with some easy duties and instruction being started in the first few days, working up to fully-fledged employee status after three to six months (depending on the work complexity and responsibilities).*

- *Internal candidates changing to a different level in an organisation also need induction. They need to know about management practices and how they should be implemented. They will have particular difficulties with a change in status.*

ACTION   Carmel decides that Joseph has not given enough priority to the new deputy manager's induction. She goes through the induction plan with him and insists that he covers all the aspects that have not already been tackled. She is especially keen that he discusses supervision and management standards with Daria as this is her weakest area.

Carmel then sees Daria herself and explains that Joseph was at fault for not arranging her induction more systematically, and for making assumptions about her ability to cope with the transition to being a deputy manager. She explains that she hopes this has not put her off management in RESCROFT and that she thinks that she will make a good deputy manager once her confidence about handling supervision and disciplinary issues is increased.

Daria explains her resentment again, but is pleased by the outcome of the meeting.

OUTCOME   Daria's probationary period is extended by a further six weeks and Joseph spends a good part of that time assisting her in management queries and working with the team to integrate her into the hierarchy and to establish her authority.

COMMENT   *Induction is too important to be ignored or left aside whether a worker is an internal or external candidate.*

NEXT STEP   Carmel amends the internal candidates policy to re-emphasise induction procedures.

TIPS ON INDUCTION

- When the terms of appointment are agreed and a start date finalised, you can plan the induction period. All new workers in an organisation benefit from an induction period. One of the main causes of staff turnover in the first year is a poor introduction to the organisation. When you have spent several thousand pounds on recruiting the right person, it doesn't make sense to alienate them from day one.
- Always plan an induction programme — ensure it is completely appropriate for the new employee.
- Alert staff to the presence of the new employee.
- Elect a 'buddy' to pair up with the new employee to answer questions as necessary. Make sure you pick one who will do the job properly.

INDUCTION FORMAT

An approach that has a standard format and checklist of things the employees must be told, combined with a focus on the actual reservations, needs and anxieties of individual employees' will be the winning one.

Apart from technical employment details like P45 etc, concentrate first on things that the employee is going to be most worried about:

- What's my line manager like?
- What are my colleagues like?
- What's the 'culture' like?
- What standards do I have to perform to?
- How long do I have to learn them in?
- Who can I ask or interrupt for help?

The main point is to give an employee confidence in their new job as soon as possible.

A 'buddy' assigned to look after a new worker in the induction period, and introduce them to colleagues and the organisation, would best not be that worker's line manager and perhaps not even in the same team.

CHECKLIST OF STEPS IN AN INDUCTION PROGRAMME

- The new worker's desk or workstation
- Their line manager
- Introduction to fellow workers
- Personnel details — P45, home details, emergency details
- Pay and benefits details, holidays and other leave arrangements (including sickness)
- Staff facilities — canteen, parking, nursery etc
- Terms of employment, disciplinary rules and grievance procedures
- General nature of the work to be done
- Detailed job description
- Relationship of post to others
- Communication procedures
- Staff handbook
- Personnel policies
- Health and safety rules
- Fire exits
- Departmental rules
- Supervision arrangements
- Probationary period format and personal attainment targets
- History of the organisation
- Follow-up

INDUCTION FOR A PERSON WITH A DISABILITY

The same content of the programme should be followed as outlined above. In addition it is good practice to carry out the following:

- Ask the new employee if they need any help and what it might be.
- Discuss whether the employee wants information about their disability given to other staff.
- Maintain confidentiality where necessary.
- Make sure that supervisors and colleagues are adequately consulted and briefed on any arrangements made with the new employee.
- Ensure a suitable car parking space if necessary.
- Give a blind person the opportunity to learn the layout of the building.
- Arrange that reception and other appropriate staff know if a new employee has a hearing or verbal communication difficulty and may prefer messages taken in writing.
- Make sure employees have somewhere private to take medication if necessary.
- Make arrangements for installing aids and adaptations or possibly for guide dogs.

31 PROBATIONARY PERIOD

Safeguarding standards

Martha, the new Information Officer at Alcohol Counselling Service (ACS), is coming up for her probationary period review. In the first three months she has been getting on well with networking and meeting people. She is working well with the team, but there have been one or two incidents that Adam has not been happy with. She has not done anything on keeping the computer database up to date. Her excuse has always been that she has got to go and meet people as a priority and the database can wait. Unfortunately there is a deadline for preparing a listing that Adam would like to take to a national conference. This listing is also something that the funders of that part of the service have been waiting for for six months. Adam is running out of excuses for them and feels he has to pressurise Martha more to get on with this side of the work.

One further worrying aspect is that some of the staff suspect that Martha is not actually using the information bank very well. She has a small area of expertise that she is very good on; but doesn't check her facts when giving information on other areas of the service. One adviser has complained to Adam of an instance of her giving incorrect advice to him that led one of his clients to try to contact a specialist counselling service that had closed down and the client was very distraught about this.

Should Adam: OPTIONS

- delay Martha's probationary interview and insist that she gets up to speed on the database so that he can assess her skills on it?
- raise the issues about her incorrect advice and lack of progress on the database in a routine supervision session?
- wait for the probationary interview and simply not confirm her in post if she is still not satisfactory in these two areas, perhaps extending the probationary period?

ISSUES
- *If you're going to use a probationary period, plan it properly and manage the performance of workers particularly closely over the period, to be fair to them and you.*
- *Be clear with yourself and the employees about the purpose and shape of the probationary period.*
- *Work out a proper programme for assessing performance.*
- *Give the worker adequate opportunity to comment on and challenge any aspects of the assessment.*
- *Where probationary periods often go wrong is when the standards of performance were not set strictly enough at the start, or the induction system is not followed rigorously enough. The worker may try to use both of these facts to argue that for confirmation in post, when that worker really is not good enough. Even if the employee is good enough, the organisation may not have the management ability to know that, or to realise if workers are being hampered from giving their best.*

PLANNING
Adam needs to own up to the fact that he has let the timetable of induction slip and so it is not Martha's fault that she has not got on with the database work. He has been so busy over the last three months that he has not had enough time to pay attention to Martha, and issues that should have come up in her supervision are not being attended to closely enough.

OUTCOME
At the end of the next month, Martha has her preliminary probationary interview and passes that. She spent a lot of time working on the database and admitted that she did have a fear of the computer technology which was slightly different from the one she had used before. She improved her information work which was a bit slipshod owing to what was common practice in her previous workplace. She was glad of the opportunity to put forward her worries and get them sorted out by a frank discussion with Adam before the pressure of the formal probationary period interview.

COMMENT
Adam recognised that he was at fault and sorted out the supervision plan necessary to enable Martha to work at her best. What could have ended in a non-confirmation of Martha in post was in fact a highly successful appointment.

NEXT STEP
Adam prepares clear targets for the next two months that he expects to be met at the final probationary interview.

TIPS ON PROBATIONARY PERIODS

- Where there are any problems in the probationary period, work out a jointly agreed programme including training, an agreed time period allowed for implementation and a proper review period and assessment carried out at the end of the period.

- Where a probationary period is not confirmed, confer the right of appeal. An appeal panel must not include anyone previously involved in assessing the performance of the worker, although evidence can be taken from such people as well as from the worker concerned. Trade union representation (where recognised) should be allowed at any appeal hearing.

- Make all written assessments of the worker's performance available to that worker and any appeal panel but this information should otherwise be kept confidential.

- Keep minutes of all meetings.

LEGAL ASPECTS OF PROBATION

Probationary periods at the start of employment have a set of legal principles attached to them. If you are going to use a probationary period you must give the employee the following details of that period:

- The purpose of the period
- Standards and review periods
- The length of the probation
- Notice provisions.

The employer has a duty to set standards of performance to be met, and provide training and feedback. If you can show that you have done this, then you can dismiss those whose performance is still unsatisfactory at the end of the period.

It is also important to put into the contract that during the probationary period either party may terminate the contract by giving very short, often seven days', notice in writing.

SAMPLE PROBATIONARY PROCEDURE

X Organisation employs all new workers on condition that they must satisfactorily complete a probationary period of three months, although this may be extended by a further three months at the request of either the worker or the line manager.

In the case of the Director, the probationary interviews will be carried out by the chair of the Board or Management Committee.

At the beginning of the period the line manager and worker will discuss the job description and agree performance standards and targets to be attained at the end of a two- and three-month period.

There will be an induction programme running alongside the probationary period.

Two months

After two months there will be a formal interview between the line manager and the worker to discuss the worker's performance and to assess whether the agreed targets have been met. The line manager will be expected to prepare a report before the meeting assessing the worker's performance and to discuss it with other senior management team members as necessary.

This report will be discussed at the interview and the worker can comment on the report and make any observations about the contents or any problems experienced in carrying out the work. The meeting will be minuted and both parties asked to sign the minutes as a true record.

If there are any problems a plan of action, including a programme of relevant training, will be agreed by both parties for review after a further month. At this point the probationary period may be extended by a further month (to four months in total) if is is felt that improvements or training could not adequately be assessed within one month. This plan of action should be fully minuted.

Three or four months

A further interview with a written report will be held for all probationers at the end of three months (or four months if the period has been extended), again fully minuted. Where there have been no problems, the worker is confirmed in post.

Where there have been problems, the plan of training and improvements is reviewed with comments from the worker. The worker is told whether the appointment is to be confirmed or the probationary period to be extended for a further period up to six months in total.

continued

SAMPLE PROBATIONARY PROCEDURE (continued)

Where the probationary period is to be extended, a further review must be held at the end of the six-month period to discuss the worker's performance. At the end of this period the worker will be formally confirmed in post or not.

Appeal

The worker may appeal against a negative decision within three working days of receipt of the formal letter of non-confirmation, to the (most relevant person) next senior line manager, personnel manager, regional manager or chair of the Management Committee and may have a trade union representative present at any appeal hearing.

The relevant person must convene an appeal hearing within ten working days of the receipt of the formal letter of non-confirmation. This will normally consist of a member of the Management Committee and a line manager who is not the probationer's manager.

The appeal committee will take notice of the minutes of all review meetings and will interview the line manager concerned and the probationer before reaching a decision. The decision of the appeal panel is final.

No one gets more than two reviews (one ideally, two in exceptional circumstances).

FURTHER READING

Where a publisher is mentioned below in **bold** the address can be found at the end of this section.

GENERAL The **Institute of Personnel and Development** Library publish a list of Information notes on various topics of interest such as sexual harassment, Aids and the Workplace, Counselling, etc.

EQUAL OPPOR-TUNITIES **General Policy Development**

Equality in Action: Introducing equal opportunities in voluntary organisations, Mee-Yan Cheung-Judge & Alix Henley, **NCVO** , 1994

Equal Opportunities: A guideline for managers, Gill Taylor, **Industrial Society**, 1994

Equal Opportunities — The Way Ahead, Jane Straw, **IPD**, 1990

Equal Opportunities at Work, Mary Coussey & Hilary Jackson, Pitman, 1991

Training: The Implementation of Equal Opportunities at Work, Volumes 1 and 2, **CRE**, 1987

From Equality to Diversity: A business case for equal opportunities, Rachel Ross & Robin Schneider, Pitman, 1992

Managing to Discriminate, David Collinson, David Knights & Margaret Collinson, Routledge, 1990

Maximising Human Resources through Equal Opportunities, **Local Government Management Board**, 1990

Breaking Through the Glass Ceilings, Lesley Abdela, Metropolitan Authorities Recruitment Agency, 1991

Equal Opportunities Review, **Industrial Relations Service**, journal published six times a year

Code of Practice on Equal Opportunities, **IPD**

Equal Opportunities: Ten point plan for employers, Employment Department Group (available from **Cambertown Ltd**)

Equal Opportunity in Voluntary Organisations Reading List No 2, **NCVO**

Black and ethnic minority people

Booklets, **Commission for Racial Equality:**
Implementing Equal Opportunity Policies
Equal Opportunity in Employment: a Guide for Employers
Monitoring an Equal Opportunity Policy: A Guide for Employers
Positive Action and Equal Opportunity in Employment
Why Keep Ethnic Records ?

Equal Opportunities: What is positive action? **Race Relations Employment Advisory Service**

Racial Discrimination and Grievance procedures: a practical guide for employers, **CRE**

Britain's Ethnic Minorities, Trevor Jones, **Policy Studies Institute,** 1993

Multi-ethnic Britain: Facts and trends, **The Runnymede Trust,** 1994

People with disabilities

Code of Practice on the Employment of Disabled People, Disability Advisory Service (available from local job centres)

Lesbians and Gay Men

Equal Opportunities for Lesbians and Gay Men; Guidelines to good practice in employment, **LAGER,** 1993

Less Equal than Others: a survey of lesbians and gay men at work, **Stonewall**

All in a Day's Work: A report on anti-lesbian discrimination in employment and unemployment in London, Ed Nina Taylor, Lesbian Employment Rights, 1986 (available from **LAGER**)

Gay Men at Work, Phil Greasley, **LAGER,** 1986

Ex-Offenders

Releasing the Potential: a guide to good practice for the employment of people with criminal records, Apex Trust, Next Step Training.

Wiping the Slate Clean (leaflet on the Rehabilitation of Offenders Act), **Home Office**

EQUALITY TARGETS, POSITIVE ACTION & MONIT- ORING

A measure of equality: Monitoring and achieving racial equality in Employment, **CRE**, 1990

We're Counting on Equality: Monitoring equal opportunities in the workplace (covers sex, race, disability, sexuality, HIV/AIDS and age) **City Centre**

RECRUITMENT, SELECTION AND APPOINTMENT

Employment Practice Guidelines, Gill Taylor, **FIAC**,1993

Job Descriptions, Gill Taylor, **FIAC** 1993

Employing Temporary, Part-time Workers and Consultants, Gill Taylor, **FIAC**, 1996

Managing People, Gill Taylor, **Directory of Social Change**, 1995

Recruitment Code, **IPD**

Code on Occupational Testing, **IPD**

Lines of Progress: an enquiry into selection tests and equal opportunities in London Underground, **CRE**, 1990

Equal Opportunity Guidelines for Best Test Practice in the Use of Personal Selection Tests, **Saville & Holdsworth**, 1991

Guidelines for Testing People with Disabilities, **Saville and Holdsworth**

CONTRACT TERMS AND CONDITIONS

ACAS guide to Discipline at work, ACAS

Croner's Reference Guides handbooks with an updating service; and booklets on key issues such as Grievance; Health and Safety, **Croner**

GEE Essential Facts, Employment, The Personnel Manager's Factbook Guides and handbooks updated by a subscriber service, **GEE**

Racial Discrimination and Grievance Procedures: a practical guide for employers, **CRE**

Managing Change

Just about Managing: A guide to effective management for voluntary organisations and community groups, Sandy Adirondack, **LVSC,** Second Edition, 1992

Managing Change in Organisations, Colin Carnall, Prentice Hall, 1990

Harassment

Sensitive Issues in the Workplace, Sue Morris, **Industrial Society,** 1993

No Offence? Sexual Harassment: How it happens and how to beat it, **Industrial Society,** 1993

Racial Discrimination and Grievance Procedures **CRE,** 1991

Sexual Harassment: information pack, **EOC**

Preventing and Remedying Sexual Harassment at Work, Michael Rubenstein, **Industrial Relations Service,** 1992

Tackling Sexism and Sexual Harassment, **City Centre**

Sexual Harassment in the Workplace: the facts employees should know, DOE, 1992

Bullying at Work: how to confront and overcome it, Andrea Adams, Virago, 1992

Statement on Harassment, **IPD**

Racial Harassment at Work, **City Centre**

FLEXIBLE WORKING

Job Sharing: employment rights and conditions, **New Ways to Work**

Fair Shares: making job shares work, Mike Rosen & Patricia Leighton, **Hackney Job Share,** 1991

Flexibility and Choice: new work patterns for the nineties, **Local Government Management Board,** 1993

New Work Patterns, Patricia Leighton & M Syrett, Pitman, 1989

THE LAW

Discrimination Law, Michael Malone, Kogan Page, 1993

Discrimination at Work: the law on sex and race discrimination, Camilla Palmer, Legal Action Group, 1992

Booklets, **Commission for Racial Equality**
  Positive Action and Equal Opportunity in Employment
  Guidelines for Advertisers and Employers : Race Relations Act 1976
  Monitoring an Equal Opportunities Policy
  Why Keep Ethnic Records ?

Booklets, **Equal Opportunities Commission**
Guidelines for Equal Opportunities Employers
Positive Action in Recruitment Advertising
The Sex Discrimination Act and Advertising
Job Evaluation Schemes Free of Sex Bias

Racial Discrimination: a guide to the Race Relations Act 1976, **Home Office**

Sex Discrimination: a guide to the Sex Discrimination Act 1975, **Home Office**

Code of Practice for the elimination of discrimination on the grounds of sex and marriage and the promotion of equality of opportunity in employment, **EOC, 1985**

Code of Practice for the elimination of racial discrimination and the promotion of equality of opportunity in employment, **CRE, 1983**

ADDRESSES **Cambertown Ltd,** Employment Department, Goldthorpe Industrial Estate, Goldthorpe, Rotherham, S63 9BC

City Centre, 32–35 Featherstone St, London EC1Y 8QX, *0171 608 1338*

CRE (Commission for Racial Equality), 10–12 Allington St, London SW1E 5EH

Croner's Law Guides, Customer Services, *0181 547 3333*

Directory of Social Change, 24 Stephenson Way, London NW1 2DP, *0171 209 5151*

EOC (Equal Opportunities Commisssion), Overseas House, Quay Street, Manchester M3 3HN, *0161 833 9244*

GEE, 21 Business Centre, Molly Millars Lane, Wokinghgam, Berks RG11 2QY, *Customer Services, 0800 289520*

Hackney Job Share, 380 Old St, London EC1V 9LT

Home Office, 50 Queen Anne's Gate, London SW1H 9AT

Industrial Relations Service, 18–20 Highbury Place, London N5 1QP, *0171 354 5858*

Industrial Society, 48 Bryanston Square, London W1H 7LN *0171 262 2401*

IPD (Institute of Personnel & Development), IPD House, Camp Road, London SW19 4UX, *0181 971 9000*

LAGER (Lesbian & Gay Employment Rights), Unit 1G, Leroy House, 436 Essex Rd, London N1 3QP, *0171 704 6066*

Local Government Management Board, Arndale House, Arndale Centre, Luton LU1 2TS, *01582 451166*

NCVO (National Council for Voluntary Organisations), Regents Wharf, 8 All Saints St, London N1 9RL, *0171 713 6161*

New Ways to Work, 309 Upper St, London N1 2TY, *0171 226 4026*

Policy Studies Institute, 110 Park Village East, London, NW1 3SR, *0171 387 2171*

Race Relations Employment Advisory Service, 11 Belgrave Road, London, SW1H 1RB

Runnymede Trust, 11 Princelet St, London E1 6QH

Saville & Holdsworth, 3 AC Court, High St, Thames Ditton, Surrey T7 0SR

Stonewall, 16 Clerkenwell Close, London, EC1R OAA, *0171 336 8860*

Exit interview report form

See Scenario 2, page 11

EXIT INTERVIEW REPORT

Name:

Post leaving:

How long in post:

How long in organisation:

Reasons for leaving:

Implications for —
    Job description:

    Person specification

    Salary level

Job re-evaluation needed?

Action taken by line manager:

Date:

Appendix II
Flexible working application form

See Scenario 4, page 17

APPLICATION FOR JOBSHARE / PART-TIME WORKING
(INTERNAL APPLICATION)

Please apply at least <u>3 months</u> before you want the new arrangement to start.

Name: Date:

Job title:

Current working hours: Regular extra hours:

I would like to be considered for the following flexible-time arrangement:
(Please tick the relevant box)

Part-time working	☐	Jobsharing	☐
Term-time working	☐	Working from home	☐
Career break	☐	Cultural/religious need	☐
Flexible leave	☐		

Please give further details of your application and your reasons:

Application agreed by line manager *(signed)*:   Date:

Reasons for refusal by line manager:

                          (signed):   Date:

Confirmed by senior manager *(signed)*:   Date:

Sample job description

See Scenario 10, page 39

JOB DESCRIPTION

Name of project:	ADVICE CENTRE
Address of project:	The Shop, High St, Anytown
Job title:	VOLUNTEER COORDINATOR
Responsible to:	Project Manager
Persons responsible for:	20 volunteers (at least 1 day per week each)
Grade (and starting salary):	SO1 (Point 29)
Working hours:	35 hours (Monday–Friday 9.00am–5.00pm, flexible according to contract terms)
Special conditions:	Evening work Local travel
Date written:	1/7/93
Current postholder started:	1/11/93

Job summary:

To recruit, train, support and develop volunteers for the Centre. To coordinate the work of volunteers at the centre.

Responsibilities:

Volunteer recruitment
- Produce and distribute publicity materials and displays to attract volunteers to the Centre.
- Undertake talks and public speaking on the work and role of the volunteers at the Centre.
- Write press releases and stimulate media coverage where appropriate.

Volunteer selection
- Recruit, interview, counsel and assess prospective volunteers.
- Ensure the above is carried out in line with the equal opportunities practice guidelines operated by the Centre.

Training and support
- Develop and monitor the training programme for volunteers. Recruit other centre staff or outside trainers for the programme as appropriate.
- Develop and monitor the use of the volunteer agreement.
- Ensure new volunteers attend training and attain standards of competence before providing advice to the public.
- Organise refresher and new courses on relevant issues.
- Provide regular support and arrange professional supervision sessions for volunteers.
- Act as a personnel manager to the volunteers at the project.
- Liaise with the Project Manager and advice team about the level of competence of the volunteers and facilitate the resolution of any difficulties between staff and volunteers.

Administration
- Organise the rotas for volunteer sessions.
- Ensure volunteers' expenses are paid in accordance with the volunteer agreement.
- Ensure all volunteers are aware of the health and safety and equal opportunities policies and guidelines and adhere to them in the course of their work.
- Collect statistics on the work of the volunteers, numbers, training and turnover.
- Prepare reports for the Management Committee on the work and future development of volunteers in the work of the advice centre.

General duties
- Attend staff meetings.
- Be self servicing.
- Participate in office rotas as necessary.
- Adhere to the project's equal opportunities policy and implement any practice guidelines in the course of duties.

Priorities may vary from time to time as the project's service delivery changes.

Sample person specification

See Scenario 11, page 42

PERSON SPECIFICATION

Name of project: National Organisation of Health Promotion Projects

Job title: DEVELOPMENT WORKER

---

1 Experience

3 years experience of health promotion work in the health service or voluntary sector at community level.

2 years experience of co-ordinating, planning and prioritising work in a small community or voluntary organisation.

Experience of training and seminar course design and delivery appropriate to health promotion work.

2 Skills and Abilities

Ability to communicate assertively with a wide range of people.

Clear written style in report writing and publicity material.

Ability to use a word-processor.

Ability to work to team priorities.

3 Knowledge

Knowledge of and commitment to the work of local health promotion campaigns.

Practical knowledge of implementing equal opportunities policies and practices.

4 Qualifications/Education/Training

No specific education or training required.

5 Other Requirements

Ability to drive (car provided).

Ability to travel in the region including occasional overnight stays.

6 Legal Requirements

None.

DESIRABLE

Experience of preparing budgets and cash flows.

Experience of public speaking.

Experience of marketing and promotion techniques relevant to the voluntary sector.

Sample application form

See Scenario 12, page 45

Registered Charity No.....

JOB APPLICATION FORM

Post applied for:

GUIDELINES FOR APPLICANTS

Please read these notes carefully before completing the application form.

You should have a job description and person specification with this application form.

Job description: The job description describes the objectives and duties of the job for which you are applying. You should check that you feel able to undertake the duties of the job before applying.

Person specification: The person specification describes the skills, experience, abilities and other factors we shall be looking for when selecting applicants. Please read this carefully and address how you fulfil each point on the specification when answering question 2 of the application form.

It is very important that you fill this in as fully and completely as possible, giving concrete evidence of skills and experience where possible.

GENERAL INFORMATION

Please use black ink. You may reproduce pages two and three on your computer and send us the pages printed off. You must not send more than three pages of typed script in answer to questions two and three. The rest of the form must be filled in by hand.

Please complete each section. CVs are not accepted.

Please make sure that we get the form by the closing date. Late applications will not be considered.

If you are shortlisted for interview, we will reimburse the cost of your travel at standard class public transport rates. If you are shortlisted for interview and have special needs for example, a BSL interpreter or nearby parking, please let us know when you receive details of your interview date and time.

EQUAL OPPORTUNITIES

This organisation is committed to equal opportunities and its managers have a duty to ensure that all recruitment decisions are based on criteria relevant to the job. We will not discriminate unfairly on the grounds of an applicant's gender, race, skin colour, nationality or ethnic origin, level of physical ability, religious belief or lack of it, marital status, sexual orientation, responsibility for dependents, age, appearance or membership of a trade union.

We monitor all applicants for employment. It would be helpful if you would complete the monitoring form included as a separate sheet with this application form. It will be kept separate from both the form and your personal details and will not be seen by the employing manager.

WORK HISTORY

Please tell us about your work history including any casual or part time work and regular or voluntary work. Also include time spent caring for dependents. Please start with your most recent work.

Employer	From	To	Work done and main duties (state if full or part time)

EXPERIENCE

The person specification lists the essential criteria necessary for doing this job. Please show how you meet each requirement, in the same order as they appear on the person specification. It is not enough simply to say you have done something, you need to say when and how the experience or skills were gained. Include any training or qualifications where relevant.

Please continue overleaf if necessary.

EXPERIENCE continued

GENERAL INFORMATION

How many days absence have you had from work in the last 12 months?

If more than 10 please give details:

If offered this post when would you be able to start?

Where did you hear about this job?

I declare that this information is correct.

Signed:
Date:

COMPLAINTS PROCEDURE

If you feel you have been discriminated against during any stage of the recruitment procedure, please write to the chair of the Management Committee via our office address. You will then be advised of the complaints procedure.

PLEASE RETURN THE FORM by:

PERSONAL DETAILS   *(To be detached from the application form)*

JOB REF:

SURNAME: FIRST NAME:

ADDRESS:

DAYTIME TEL: EVENING TEL:

Please give details of two referees. One referee must be your current or most recent employer. References will only be taken up if you are shortlisted and with your permission.

Name: Address: Telephone:

1.

2.

If your previous employers no longer exist, or if there have been breaks in your employment over the last three years, please give the name of a responsible person to act as a personal referee. Your personal referee must not be related to you and must have known you for the last three years.

EQUAL OPPORTUNITIES MONITORING FORM

JOB REF:

This monitoring information will help us check if our advertising is reaching all sections of the community and that the final selection decision was made on fair grounds. All information will be held in strict confidence.

Gender: Male ☐   Female ☐

Age: Less than 35 ☐   35–49 ☐   over 50 ☐

Do you consider yourself to have a disability?

Ethnic Origin: This section uses the same categories as in the latest government census. We are therefore able to monitor if applications reflect the local population. What do you regard as your ethnic origin?

White ☐   Black Caribbean ☐   Black African ☐   Black other [please specify]

Pakistani ☐   Bangladeshi ☐   Chinese ☐   Other [please specify]

PLEASE TURN OVER

[This is the other side of the Personal details form]

NOTICE TO APPLICANTS

If you are applying for work directly with young people, the provisions of the Rehabilitation of Offenders Act do not apply. This means that you are not entitled to withhold information about convictions which, for other purposes are 'spent' under the provision of the Act. Failure to disclose such convictions could result in your dismissal at a later date. Information will be treated as confidential and will be considered only in relation to applications for positions to which the order applies.

Have you ever been convicted of criminal offences?

If yes give brief details below or in a sealed envelope marked for the attention of the director and send with this form.

I understand that if I have used misleading information to gain employment with this organisation then I may be instantly dismissed at a later date.

Signed: Date

Equal opportunities monitoring form

See Scenario 16, page 57

[See also the example of a monitoring form attached to the sample application form.]

EQUAL OPPORTUNITIES MONITORING

Application number:

We aim to be an equal opportunity employer and select staff solely on merit irrespective of race, sex, disability, sexuality, etc. In order to monitor the effectiveness of our equal opportunity policy we ask all applicants to provide the information below. This will be kept confidential to the selection panel and will be seen by them only after the shortlisting has been completed.

The information will not be used as part of the selection process itself and is held confidentially and anonymously, separate from the main body of the application forms, until after the shortlisting process.

Name: Phone number:

Address:

1   Are you MALE/FEMALE?

2   Do you have a disability?   YES/NO

3   What is your date of birth?

4   How would you describe your ethnic origin?
    African-Caribbean ☐   Asian (including East African Asian) ☐
    Cypriot (Greek/Turkish) ☐   Chinese ☐   Vietnamese ☐
    Irish ☐   White ☐   Other (please specify):

5   Would you describe yourself as:
    Heterosexual ☐   Bisexual ☐   Lesbian or gay ☐

6   Post applied for?

7   Where did you see this job advertised?

Sample covering letter

See Scenario 17, page 60

Date

Dear Enquirer,

JOB TITLE

Thank you for your enquiry about this post.

Please find enclosed:
— a job description and person specification
— an application form
— general information about the job
— the project's core aims and purpose
— the project's equal opportunities policy

An equal opportunities monitoring form is included as part of the application form. It will be detached upon receipt and the information used only as part of a monitoring process (and not as part of the selection procedure).

Applicants will be shortlisted according to how well they meet the criteria in the person specification. Please explain on the application form how you meet the criteria. Please do not include a CV.

All application forms will be acknowledged and you will be informed by post whether you have been shortlisted or not.

Interviews will take place in .... on ....

We look forward to receiving your application by .... at the latest.

Yours sincerely,

Manager

This organisation is a Registered Charity.

Shortlisting marking form

See Scenario 19, page 66

SHORTLISTING MARKING FORM	Panel member:		
	Page no:	Date:	

Skills, etc, from person specification:	Applicants' ref numbers and scores on each item:														
Total scores:															

Best candidates:	
1	
2	
3	
4	

Guidelines for marking:

0 = no evidence
1 = limited evidence
2 = average
3 = very good

Example of prepared questions

Scenario 24, page 83

Part-time adviser post — Interview questions

Introduction
- Welcome
- Introductions
- Length of interview
- Questions at end
- Same questions to all
- Note taking
- Discuss case study

1. **Bearing in mind the job description, how can you relate your previous experience to this job?**

2. **From your experience, what are the issues affecting people living in the inner-cities?**

   (Poverty, housing, transport, health, racism, homelessness, communication unemployment, lack of opportunities, access, transport, isolation)

3. **What skills and qualities do you think are important in a good advice worker?**

   (Listening, discovering what the client wants, non-judgmental, clear boundaries, sympathy, respect, sensitivity, ability to ask relevant questions, good knowledge of area of work, good communications skills, helping clients to help themselves)

4. **This is a job where you will need to work under pressure and with a heavy workload. What are your own strategies for dealing with this?**

   (Prioritisation, recognising stress, able to admit difficulties, ability to ask for help, time management, realistic goals)

---

5. **How do you implement equal opportunities in your day to day work? Please give us some examples.**

   (Language, access, publicity , targeting, monitoring, review, thinking about individual needs, awareness of needs, research, training, good policy and procedures, knowledge of the effects of discrimination, networking)

6. **Case study**

   A. What would you advise them to do?

   (Homeless application to HPU on ground of unsuitable accommodation; explain previous abuse and present overcrowding; challenge attempt to declare intentionally homeless; investigate why council have not acted on racial abuse)

   B. What advice would you give him?

   (Pay in lieu of notice; redundancy pay; accrued holiday pay; written reasons for dismissal; unfair dismissal; application to IT within 3 months)

   C. What advice would you give him?

   (Not entitled to HB — living with relative)

   D. What advice would you give him?

   (Partner signs on and claims IS for family; voluntary unemployment suspension of benefit will not apply; partner has to be available for work)

7. **What tactics would you use to ensure that our services are used by all the local communities?**

   (Good visual publicity, translated as appropriate, targeting, talks, networking with other organisations, needs of all groups, enabling access, interpreting facilities)

8. **A client comes into the advice centre and makes a complaint about the behaviour of his neighbour. He tells you that the neighbour is a loony and shouldn't be living there. What do you ask him?**

   (What is the actual complaint?)

9. **What are the advantages and disadvantages of working in a team?**

   (Support, sharing skills and information, shared responsibilities, alleviate isolation, increase knowledge of other areas of work, take part in decision-making, stress levels reduced)

   (Lack of communication, disagreements, lack of clear decision-making, things take longer, isolation, different priorities, power imbalances)

10. **If offered the job, when could you start?**

11. **What days, other than Wednesday mornings, are you available to work?**

12. **Assess verbal presentation**

Conclusion
   Are there any questions you would like to ask us?
   Expenses
   Let you know by early next week

Interviewer:

Interview marking form

See Scenario 26, page 90

INTERVIEW MARKING FORM

Panel member:	
Page no:	Date:

Essential skills, etc, from person specification:	Candidates' names and scores on each requirement:					
Totals (panel member 1):						
Totals (panel member 2):						
Totals (panel member 3):						
Totals (panel member 4):						
Total scores:						
Chosen candidate:			Reserve:			

Appendix XI
Sample reference request

See Scenario 27, page 94

Date

Dear [name],

<u>Reference for [name] of [address]</u>

I am writing to request a written reference for [name], who has been selected (pending successful references) for the post of [job title] (job description enclosed) at _____ and has given your name as a referee.

Could you confirm that they have been working for you as _____ since _____.

I should like to ask you to provide a detailed reference as to how well in your view or experience the above person meets the criteria on the person specification included with this letter. Could you cover each criterion separately please?

If you feel you cannot comment on any point, please say why, briefly.

I should also like to know how many days' sick leave [name] has taken over the last year, and whether they were spread out or consecutive.

If you would like to discuss any of these points please telephone me at the above number.

I should be obliged if you could give this a high priority as we cannot make the appointment until all references have been received.

I enclose a stamped addressed envelope for your reply.

Yours sincerely,

    Chair of the Selection Panel
    [Line Manager]

Encs: Job description
      Person Specification

Appendix XII

Sample offer letter

See Scenario 28, page 98

Date

Dear [name],

[Job title]

I am writing to confirm formally that _____ would like to offer you the post of [job title], subject to the receipt of satisfactory written references.

I enclose a copy of the contract of employment that operates at _____ which you will be required to sign should you decide to take up our offer of employment.

[Fixed-term or temporary contract details should be included here]

Your initial salary will be _____ and this is increased each year by a cost of living award and length of service up to a bar at _____ .

You have to be in post for six months to qualify for the increment which takes place on 1 April annually.

The hours of work are 9.00am–5.00pm Monday to Friday, with one hour for lunch, subject to flexitime rules laid out in the contract and discussion with your line manager. [Add time off in lieu or paid overtime rules.]

[Mention the points below where relevant]

Holiday entitlement

Pension scheme

Car or car loan

Travel or season ticket loan

Professional subscriptions paid

Access to training and paid relevant professional qualifications training

Childcare scheme

continued

Any maternity or paternity leave which is above the statutory minimum

Any other working arrangements that are beneficial to carers or parents

We operate a probationary period of four months, extendible by a further two months, if necessary, for all new employees. During the probationary period either party may terminate the contract by giving seven days' notice in writing. Once this has been completed satisfactorily you will be confirmed in post.

I would be grateful if you would contact me at the office as soon as possible to confirm your acceptance of the offer. If I have not heard from you by _____ I will assume that you are no longer interested in the post.

I look forward to hearing from you.

Yours sincerely,

Chair of Selection Panel [Director or Chair of Management Committee]

Sample rejection letter

See Scenario 29, page 101

Date

Dear [name]

[Job title]

Thank you for coming to the interview for the post of job title, [whenever].

The panel was impressed by _____ [something].

However, unfortunately we are not able to offer you the job. The standard of applicants was high and there were others who fully met more of the essential person specification criteria than you did.

I am sorry to write to you with this news. If you require more information about the decision please get in touch with the [Line Manager] on [telephone number].

I can also arrange for you to have details of the decision in writing should you wish it.

I would like to wish you luck in any future job applications you may be making.

Yours sincerely,

[Chair of the Selection Panel]
